THE STORY

Grasping the Metanarrative
in a Postmodern World

BY JEFF REED

© Jeff Reed, 2016

All rights reserved. No part of this publication may be reproduced, stored in a retrieval system, or transmitted in any form or by any means (electronic, mechanical, photocopy, recording, or any other) except for brief quotations in printed reviews, without the prior permission of the publisher.

Published by BILD International, Ames, Iowa 50014. BILD International resources are designed to help churches train leaders.

Art Direction & Design: Nathan Haila

All Scripture, unless otherwise noted, is from the New Revised Standard Version Bible.

ISBN 978-0-99101852-1-7

TABLE OF CONTENTS

05 THE STORY: GRASPING THE METANARRATIVE IN A POSTMODERN WORLD:

08 DESIGN OF THE STUDY GUIDE

11 SESSION 1 — THE STORYLINE

26 SESSION 2 — UNDERSTANDING THE SCRIPTURES

42 SESSION 3 — THE OVERALL PLAN

52 SESSION 4 — THE NATION OF ISRAEL

61 SESSION 5 — THE DAVIDIC COVENANT

73 SESSION 6 — THE KINGDOM ARRIVES

85 SESSION 7 — THE KINGDOM LAUNCHED

98 SESSION 8 — THE CHURCH AS CHRIST'S GRAND STRATEGY

112 SESSION 9 — THE KINGDOM FULLY REALIZED

128 SESSION 10 — RESHAPING OUR LIVES

134 ENDNOTES

135 GLOSSARY OF KEY BIBLICAL TERMS AND CONCEPTS

138 LIFELONG LEARNING

AP.
Appendix A: The Unfolding Grand Strategy - 140
Appendix B: The Story: Testimonies - 144
Appendix C: Map of Abraham's Journey - 166

PREFACE—ON THE ROAD TO EMMAUS

Imagine you were listening in to Jesus' conversation with two of His disciples on the road to Emmaus just after His resurrection. What did He say to the disciples? Why is it key for all Christians to listen in on that conversation? Luke records the essence of that conversation—a conversation that will open the Scriptures to all those desiring to follow Jesus, just as it did for the early followers after His resurrection. Let's listen in....

> 24:13 Now on that same day two of them were going to a village called Emmaus, about seven miles from Jerusalem, [14] and talking with each other about all these things that had happened. [15] While they were talking and discussing, Jesus himself came near and went with them, [16] but their eyes were kept from recognizing him.

As the conversation unfolded, it was clear that they did not grasp the significance of what had happened. Expressing His frustration, Jesus finally responded with His explanation of the significance of what His death and resurrection were really all about.

> [25] "Oh, how foolish you are, and how slow of heart to believe all that the prophets have declared! [26] Was it not necessary that the Messiah should suffer these things and then enter into his glory?" [27] Then beginning with Moses and all the prophets, he interpreted to them the things about himself in all the scriptures.

In a subsequent conversation with all the disciples before His ascension, He spoke of opening their minds to the entire Jewish Scriptures.

> [44] Then he said to them, "These are my words that I spoke to you while I was still with you—that everything written about me in the law of Moses, the prophets, and the psalms must be fulfilled." [45] Then he opened their minds to understand the scriptures....

He opened up the Scriptures to them—the Law, the Prophets, and the Psalms, in other words, the entire understanding of the Old Testament Scriptures. In this study, we are going to walk along with Jesus. You will enter into that same conversation. You will know what Jesus told these disciples that opened their entire understanding of the Scriptures. You will discover the key to understanding the Scriptures, as explained by Jesus Himself.

What will this do for you? You will understand the Story of the Bible—the entire plan of God for the world. Not only will you understand the plan itself and how it explains all of history and even man's purpose, but it will lead you to an understanding of how your life fits into that plan.

So let's walk together, with Jesus, on this road to Emmaus.

Jeff Reed,
November, 2016

THE STORY: GRASPING THE METANARRATIVE IN A POSTMODERN WORLD— INTRODUCTION

We live in a *postmodern world*. But what does that really mean? In the West, it means that no one knows the answer to life, and no one can put the world together or explain the purpose of man or understand the unfolding of history. In the West, we assume science has disproved religion, so we live in a scientific world, without religion, and no real answers. We all create our own world, the best we can. Maybe our belief is in a political system, a philosophical school, or a cause of some type, but those cannot put the world back together again after the collapse of modernism with the devastating world wars of the 20th century. Maybe we believe in a religion, but science has so neutered the supernatural in culture that often those who believe really live their lives in the secular. There is little confidence or understanding that God's metanarrative, *the Story*, is real. Even as Christians, we do not see all history through the eyes of the Story. We do not see our purpose or our culture and governmental systems through the eyes of the Story. We know we cannot live without our faith, but we cannot truly defend it in a postmodern, Western, secular culture. If we do not understand God's Story, His view of history and governments, we may even make the mistake of assuming, as do most of Islam and Western Christianity, that we can accomplish God's purposes through a religious agenda. We "believe," because we instinctively cannot live with the "malaise of modernity," as described in Charles Taylor's book *A Secular Age* (Harvard University Press, 2007). We know the spiritual realm exists, but we cannot marry the two worlds of the secular and the spiritual—the *immanent* and the *transcendent*.

If you live in the Global South (Latin America, Africa, and Asia), you live in a premodern–postmodern world. Twenty percent are educated, built on the Western university system, so are essentially postmodern and thus increasingly live in a postmodern world. Eighty percent live in a premodern world, without the benefit of 500 years of Western modern science and history; therefore, they have an untested metanarrative, based on a mixture of religious and cultural beliefs. With globalization and technology, the world is opening up to them, often through satellites on top of their shanties or village huts, but without the foundation to interpret much of what they are seeing. Enter Huntington's book *The Clash of Civilizations and the Remaking of World Order* (Simon and Schuster, 1996), which convincingly demonstrates that the 21st century will be a clash of world religions. Thus, for multiple reasons, the four billion in the world at the bottom of the pyramid, outside the Western system, will be called to accept one of the world religions, again without the chance to clearly hear God's metanarrative and be able to make a clear choice. They may accept Christianity, but without understanding God's metanarrative accurately, they will simply assimilate their new Christian beliefs into their current beliefs based upon their superstitious religious beliefs and cultural heritage (syncretism). Following their belief to truly follow Christ, they need to understand the Story and then grow in their faith and education in culture to strengthen their faith over the years.

In this study, *The Story: Grasping the Metanarrative in a Postmodern World*, we will carefully and accurately study, in just a few weeks, God's Story, as revealed in the Scriptures, as interpreted by Jesus and His Apostles. This study is useful to both postmoderns and premoderns. For postmoderns, who are open to the *transcendent*—to there being more than just what we can prove with science in a secular age—the Story will ring true with history, and it will "hold water" the more they grow in their faith. For premoderns who embrace Christ as they hear about Him, the Story will ring true as they grow in their faith and are given opportunities to become literate and have resulting educational opportunities.

The design of this study is effective with both postmoderns and premoderns, though at first that would not seem to be the case. This should not be surprising since both literates and nonliterates learned together in the early churches. They both accepted Christ, learned the Story, and grew in their faith together. But specifically, two methods built into this study booklet make it possible for both postmoderns and premoderns, both literate and non-literates, to learn together. First, we use the "walk-through" method of laying out the Story in a room. Then, using hand signals and word cues, the Story is acted out, and the historical books of the Old Testament Scriptures and related books are all hung on the storyline. Everyone learns it orally together. Second, is the design of the booklet itself. We will use "Socratic discussion" to discuss the main passages of the storyline together, which is the method Jesus and the Apostles used. "Socratic" come from Socrates' day, when he needed to bridge the gap between the literate and nonliterate Greeks. Many of the books of the Scriptures were written for nonliterates to memorize, so in a sense, these methods are not new.

To aid in the use of this study with semiliterates and nonliterates, an Easy English edition will be produced, using the method of Wycliffe Associates, UK. It will serve as the basis for translated editions in other languages. In addition, an oral edition will be produced for oral learners to listen to and study.

How do we know the Story as told and unfolded in this booklet is accurate? We followed a very simple process (though followed by long-term and advanced study) that follows the process of Jesus and His disciples ("the way of Christ and His Apostles"). We started on the road to Emmaus, when Jesus set the storyline, walking His disciples through the

Scriptures—the Law, the Prophets, and the Writings. We recreated the Story by how the Apostles told and defended it, beginning with Peter's five sermons in Acts. From their use of the Scriptures, we recreated the key passages they used again and again to tell the Story (see Appendix: "The Walk Through as the Story: The Keygmatic Framework"). We used C. H. Dodd's *According to the Scriptures: The Sub-Structure of New Testament Theology* (Fontana Books, 1965) as our key research work. The research is explained more completely in, *Teaching The Story*, a training manual that complements this study.

This study will serve a dual purpose in the BILD training system. It will serve as the foundation for *The First Principles Series*, a 13-booklet series designed to establish believers in the first principles of the faith. It will also serve as the introduction to the *Mastering the Scriptures Series*, a multi-volume, multi-year program designed for a lifelong mastery of the Scriptures.

So we invite you to join us, with Jesus, on the road to Emmaus. We invite you into a process that will open your mind to understanding the Scriptures, to understanding God's plan for building His Church and His kingdom, to understanding the meaning and purpose of your life, and to laying foundations for being a true, lifelong follower of Jesus.

DESIGN OF THE STUDY GUIDE

This study is designed to lead you through a learning process—a process designed to teach you to think. This process is based upon the Hebrew wisdom model in the Bible (the Bible's educational literature) and on sound, contemporary, educational research. It is used in all of BILD's courses, so once you have mastered the process it will serve you for all of your future work in this guide and subsequent series. It will also provide a natural study model that you can apply to all areas of your life.

Throughout nine weeks, you will follow a four-step study process. The tenth week is a summary session and final step. You will "pull together" all of your work from the nine weeks into a final project and share it in your small group.

Consistent Study Process (CSP)

A Consistent Study Process (CSP) is used ito take you through a complete learning cycle every time you study a passage or concept in the Scriptures. CSP can also serve as a convenient reminder that Bible study is not ESP—we are not trying to mystically experience the text, but to carefully and soundly study the text. There are four basic steps to this process and one final step that integrates the work from the first four.

The First Nine Weeks:

In the first nine sessions, four basic steps will be done each week: (1) Study the Scriptures, (2) Consult the Scholars, (3) Think Through the Issues, and (4) Apply the Principles.

The importance of each step is explained below.

Study the Scriptures

This step is foundational. We cannot begin exploring the issues of the Bible without first understanding exactly what the passages mean. Discussion groups in which everyone simply shares his opinion are disrespectful of the Scriptures, and therefore to God. They are often merely a pooling of ignorance.

You will go through this same first step in every session. You will begin with a passage to read, answer a few basic questions about the passage, and finally summarize the core teaching of the passage.

Your work in this step:
- Read the passage.
- Think through the questions.
- Summarize the core teaching of the passage.

Consult the Scholars

This step is very important as well, although it is not always highly valued by Christians in our generation. God raises up teachers and scholars to serve in every generation. These teachers can do great harm or great good to churches. We have provided you with some solid, carefully chosen research—in nugget form—to stimulate your thinking. These nuggets of research take two forms. One is a brief commentary on the passage. The other consists of several short instructional quotes on the ideas related to the core truths of the passage.

Your work in this step:
- Read and reflect on the brief commentary.
- Read and reflect on the key quotes.
- Record any insights from the readings.

Think Through the Issues

This step is designed to help you think through the implications of the core teaching of the passage you have been studying. Unless we go through this process, we can gloss over the significance of the core truths—the first principles of the faith. This is best done in a small group where issues can be discussed thoroughly. Debate an issue in light of the biblical text and try to come to one conclusion as a group. It is not a time for airing opinions but for genuine interaction with the issues.

Your work in this step:
- Think through the issue before discussion.
- Record your initial thoughts on the issue before discussion.
- Discuss the issue in your small group.
- Record your final thoughts after the discussion.

Apply the Principles

This step brings the basic learning cycle to completion. It is not enough to gain a clear grasp of an issue. It is not enough to accurately understand the core truths of a passage or verse in the Bible. We must apply it to our lives. Applications should be specific and related to the core truths of the passages studied.

Your work in this step:
- Think back through the first three steps.
- Design an application for your life.

The Final Session: Resphaping Our Lives:
The last session in each study guide is the final step.

Reshaping Our Lives

This step brings together the entire study process. In each of the first nine weeks, we moved through the 4-step Consistent Study Process (CSP). Now in the tenth week, you will pull together all of your work and evaluate your whole life.

Too often today, we stop short of what is necessary to really change our lives. Thinking through simple applications is very important as we study the Bible, but thinking through our whole lives in light of these new truths is essential. The final step in the study process requires that we rethink our entire lives in light of the truths we have been studying—that we rearrange our worldview. We must allow the truths to reshape every aspect of our lives.

Your work in this step:
- Commit your heart—by reflection, personal journaling, and prayer.
- Commit your mind—by forming clear convictions and memorizing Scripture.
- Commit your life—by decisions, personal projects, and life habits.

Two Final Parts of the Study Guides:
Each study booklet contains two additional parts—a glossary and a lifelong learning section.

Glossary of Key Biblical Terms and Concepts—The glossary is designed to help you with important terms that you may have encountered for the first time in your study. They are kept to a minimum in the guide, but it is not possible or preferable to remove all terms with special meaning. New terms—especially biblical terms full of rich truths—just have to be learned. To make this process easier, we have included a glossary.

Lifelong Learning—This final section introduces you to additional resources you may want to pursue. After completing a study guide, it is crucial that you do not view yourself as finished. You must understand that you are laying foundations for a lifetime of learning. Several resources are recommended for your further development.

THE STORYLINE ❶

On the Road to Emmaus, when Jesus caught up with two of His disciples and they didn't recognize Him, they were talking about the events that had just happened to Jesus. They clearly didn't understand the significance of what had just happened. He began talking to them about Moses and the Prophets. In doing so, He was reshaping their understanding of the storyline of the Scriptures.

Luke does not give us Jesus' explanation to the disciples on the road to Emmaus, but in the book of Acts, he does choose to include the speeches by Peter, Stephen, and Paul, in which they started with Moses and the Prophets and opened the Scriptures, just as Jesus did. Peter alludes to all parts of the Story in his five sermons in Acts. But it is Stephen's speech to the Jewish leaders in Jerusalem (53 verses) and Paul's speech in the Jewish synagogue at Antioch Pisidia on his first missionary journey (26 verses) that give the fullest explanation of the storyline.

In this section, we are going to recreate the storyline based on how the Apostles told the Story, after Jesus opened their minds to an accurate understanding of the Scriptures when He interpreted it for them after His resurrection. Peter's starting point was Genesis 12:1–3, as was Stephen's. Paul quickly moved to David. All gave the essence of the storyline that Jesus gave on the road to Emmaus, as they began with the Law and the Prophets. In this section, we will recreate the storyline as told by Jesus and His disciples.

Study the Scriptures

READ THE PASSAGES: ACTS 3:11–26; 7:1–53; 13:13–41

Think Through the Questions:

1. Where is the main point of the Story to be found? What are the three parts of the Scriptures? What does each main section include?
2. What are the high points of the Story?
3. In what way are Peter, Stephen, and Paul telling the same Story?
4. Why are Peter's, Stephen's, and Paul's stories a good place to begin in recreating the storyline Jesus explained on the road to Damascus?

Summarize the Core Teaching of the Passages:

Write a paragraph, outline, annotate, or chart your conclusions—whatever best communicates for you. Summarize the main points of the storyline in a way that will help tell the Story to others.

Core teaching of Acts 3:11–26; 7:1–53; 13:13–41:

Consult the Scholars

The following comments are designed to help you better understand the passage and to stimulate your thinking on the implications of the teaching.

Read and Reflect on this Brief Commentary on Acts 3:11–26; 7:1–53; 13:13–41

Three Apostolic Storylines

Each of the disciples—Peter, Stephen, and Paul—begin at the same point, the promise given to the Jews' ancestors. They all go back to Genesis 12:1–3.

Peter begins his speech by referring to the God of Abraham, Isaac, and Jacob and finishes his speech with a quote, Genesis 12:1–3: "And in your descendants all the families of the earth will be blessed."

Stephen begins with the story of Abraham. Embedded in it is the promise given to Abraham and his descendants from Genesis 12:1–3.

While Paul picks up the Story majoring on David, he begins with the fact that God chose the Jews' ancestors, and He made a great nation out of them, as promised, while they were enslaved in Egypt.

The point is they all began the Story in the same place. Stephen gives us a more detailed storyline, so we will review it first. Then we will look at Paul's storyline, since it is extensive also.

Stephen's Storyline (Acts 7:1–53)

Stephen's storyline has 4 movements:

Movement 1: From Abraham to Joseph

Movement 2: From Joseph to Moses

Movement 3: From Moses to David (and Solomon)

Movement 4: From David to the Prophets

Though Stephen does not develop the Prophets, he lumps them into a section that illustrates the nation of Israel rejected the plan God delivered to them through the prophets; they rejected all the prophets God sent them. How does he use the Prophets? He quotes from them twice to illustrate that the nation constantly rejected God's plan. The ultimate rejection was the promised Prophet, whom Moses spoke of, who would bring fulfillment to the promise given to Abraham and his descendants to bless all the families of the earth.

Paul's Storyline (Acts 13:13–41)

Paul's storyline is the same, but with a different emphasis. He quickly passes by the beginning of the Story, just referring to the Jews' ancestors—but they all knew who they were. God chose Israel and promised to make a great nation out of them. He did as He promised. They grew to be a great nation when they were in captivity in Egypt. The people rejected God's plan and didn't enter the land, thus they wandered in the wilderness for forty years. Then God gave them judges, and after demanding a king God gave them their first king, Saul. Then God replaced Saul with David who was after God's own heart, willing to follow all of His plan. From David's line came the Savior Jesus. He sent John the Baptist to announce the coming of this promised one.

Then Paul addresses the Jews of the synagogue directly, calling them the descendants of Abraham's family. He states that the leaders of Israel did not understand the very words of the Prophets they read every Sabbath and killed Jesus, but God raised Him up. He then quotes from two Psalms that predicted Jesus would rise from the dead. He ends with a quote from the Prophets warning the Jews of the synagogue not to wind up missing the great thing God is doing now!

The Composite Apostolic Storyline: The Old Testament Walk Through, Part 1

All three men—Peter, Stephen, and Paul—followed the same storyline. They each followed the storyline but selected different warnings and promises that point everything to Jesus, the coming Messiah. That is the pattern we will follow in this study. In this session we will follow the storyline. Then in sessions 3–9 we will do just as the disciples did: dip into parts of the Story with different key passages from the Scriptures for a more in-depth look at how they all point to the Messiah.

Hopefully most of you will be able to memorize the storyline by the unique way this section is intended to be taught, led by a leader. How to teach this session will be in the accompanying booklet, *How to Teach the Story*. However, if you do not have a leader teaching the storyline in this fun way, then you can just read the commentary, and it will get you up to speed. This commentary lists the main points of the Story for a leader to memorize, to lead the group from point to point. We have italicized and underlined the parts of the Story for participants to memorize and give in response. Both parts of the Review are memorized exactly so the whole group can go through the Story together. This method is for both literate and nonliterate learners.

Jesus opened the minds of the two disciples on the road to Emmaus because they had missed the point of the big Story. The following is the Story Jesus told to the disciples on the road to Emmaus, as recreated from how His disciples then told the Story. It is the heart of the Jewish Scriptures, now called the Old Testament. When Jesus turned to the Scriptures—the Law, the Prophets and the Writings—this is the Story He was interpreting for the two disciples on the road to Emmaus, as He opened their minds to understand how all of the Story pointed to Him and His kingdom. So here is the storyline in brief—a walk through of the Scriptures—with all the essential main elements of the Story.

The Backdrop to the Story: From Creation to Abraham

Genesis 1–11 serves as the backdrop to the Story, and situates it in the larger plan of God to restore man back to Himself. While it is foundational, and will be used by John in Revelation to show how God will accomplish restoring creation to His original plan, it serves as an introduction at this time. The backdrop: God, in eternity past, created the heavens and the earth. This is recorded in Genesis 1 and 2. Then the fall of man occured in Genesis 3, when Adam and Eve disobeyed God and ate from the tree of good and evil. Cain murdered Abel in Genesis 4. Evil continued to develop, and God destroyed all mankind in the great flood but preserved Noah and his family. They then re-populated the world—all in Genesis 6–8. There are genealogies in Genesis 5 and 10 tracing Adam to Noah to Abraham, which begins the story of Israel. The first 11 chapters of Genesis serve as background, situating God's focus on choosing Abraham, who would become the father of the nation of Israel, thus beginning our Story—God's plan to restore man to Himself and set up His future kingdom through Abraham and his descendants.

We will begin by telling the Story in a way that sets up all the key passages Jesus used to open the minds of the disciples to understand the Scriptures. The instructions below would be used by a teacher who is actually conducting a Walk Through of the storyline during the meeting time with those in the class. Ideally it would be done in an informal setting—a living room of a home, outdoors (in some oral settings), or some other informal setting. If there isn't a teacher to lead the Walk Through, read the storyline and memorize the underlined responses in the Review sections.[1]

The Map of Israel (The Storyline's Geographical Context)

Before we begin walking through the storyline itself, we need to lay out a map of the Old Testament geography so that we can situate the stories and characters in their setting. We will start by establishing <u>North</u>, <u>South</u>, <u>East</u>, and <u>West</u> on our map. Then we will establish the four corners of the map. In the NW corner is the <u>Black Sea</u>, in the NE corner is the <u>Caspian Sea</u>; in the SE corner is the <u>Persian Gulf</u> and in the SW corner is the country of <u>Egypt</u>. Along the West side of our map we have the <u>Mediterranean Sea</u>. There are two major rivers on our map. The first is the <u>Euphrates River</u> which flows NW. Alongside the Euphrates River flows the <u>Tigris River</u>. The land surrounding the two rivers is called the <u>Fertile Crescent</u>, which most believe is where the Garden of Eden was located. (Today, this is the area of Iraq where ISIS started; and ISIS controls the two rivers.) The land along the Mediterranean Sea where most of our action will take place is <u>Canaan</u>. A little sea just east of the Mediterranean Sea is the <u>Sea of Galilee</u>, where many Bible stories took place. Out of it flows the <u>Jordan River</u>, which dumps into the <u>Dead Sea</u>, and beyond it is the <u>Red Sea</u>.

Before you start to walk through the storyline, review.

>   **Review:**
>
>   What direction is this? <u>North</u>
>   What direction is this? <u>South</u>
>   And this? <u>East</u>
>   And this? <u>West</u>
>   In this corner we have the <u>Black Sea</u>
>   In this corner? <u>Caspian Sea</u>
>   In this corner? <u>Persian Gulf</u>
>   And in this corner? <u>Egypt</u>
>   Along the West we have what big sea? <u>the Mediterranean</u>
>   We have two major rivers: <u>the Euphrates</u>
>   and next to it? <u>the Tigris</u>
>   The land around the two rivers? <u>the Fertile Crescent</u>
>   The land where most of our story takes place <u>Canaan</u>
>   The famous sea here in the land? <u>Sea of Galilee</u>
>   Out of it flows? <u>the Jordan River</u>
>   Which dumps into what Sea? <u>the Dead Sea</u>
>   And beyond it is <u>The Red Sea</u>

The Story Jesus Told

From Abraham to Joseph

Just as with Stephen's sermon in Acts 7, our Story begins with Abraham and his family. Abraham was chosen by God to be the father of many nations. He was born in Ur of the Chaldeans so our story starts in Ur. God told him to leave Ur to go to a place He would show him. So Abraham leaves Ur with his family: his wife Sarah, his father Terah, and his nephew Lot. Thus the four main characters are Abraham, Sarah, Terah, and Lot. They leave and travel up the Euphrates River, because it was the trade route, until they come to the town of Haran, where they live for 23 years and become very rich. Terah dies at Haran. Then Abraham, Sarah, and Lot go SW to the land of Canaan, and settle there. God promises Abraham three things: land (Israel today), descendants (a great nation will come from his line) and blessing (through Abraham, God will eventually bless all the nations). Abraham had two sons, Ishmael and Isaac. Isaac had two sons: Jacob and Esau. Jacob had 12 sons. The second to the youngest was Joseph.

> **Review**
>
> Our Story starts in what town? Ur
> Our 4 main characters are? Abraham, Sarah, Terah and Lot
> God tells them to leave, so they go up what river? Euphrates
> For what reason? It was a trade route
> Until they come to what town? Haran
> Where who dies? Terah
> They leave Haran and go into what land? Canaan
> where God promises Abraham three things: land, descendants, and blessing
> Abraham had two sons: Ishmael and Isaac
> Issac had two sons: Jacob and Esau
> Jacob had how many sons? 12
> The second to the youngest was? Joseph

From Joseph to Moses

The Story now focuses on Joseph. It is through Joseph that God will begin to fulfill his promise to Abraham and his descendants to make them a great nation. This comes about in an unusual way through the life of Joseph, who was willing to follow God's unfolding plan. Joseph was his father Jacob's favorite son, his second youngest. He bestowed on him a coat of many colors. Jacob's older brothers all hated him and sold him into slavery in the country of Egypt, in the house of Potiphar, one of Pharaoh's officials, the captain of the guard. There he rose to manager over Potiphar's house, but Potiphar's wife tried to seduce him, then she lied about him, and Joseph wound up in prison. Joseph rose to the top in prison, where he was put in charge over all the prisoners. He eventually interprets Pharaoh's dream of a coming famine and was put over Pharaoh's house. He literally became second in command to Pharaoh. Through a number of circumstances,

Joseph brings his family down to Egypt, sparing them of the famine. Jacob blesses his sons, and dies. The key to Joseph's success was summed up in some of his closing words to his brothers, "You meant evil against me, but God meant it for good." Through Joseph God preserved Abraham's lineage and grew Israel into a great nation, 2^1/$_2$ million people. After Joseph dies, a new Pharaoh takes over who did not know Joseph, and he was afraid of the large number of Israelites, so he put them into slavery. We call this the 400-year Egyptian captivity.

Review

Joseph was favored by his father, hated by his brothers, so he was: sold into slavery
in the country of: *Egypt*
in the house of *Potiphar*
where he eventually becomes *second in command* over all of Eygpt.
There Israel grew into: *a great nation*; how many? *2 1/2 million people*
Joseph dies, a new Pharaoh takes over, and we have the: *400-year Egyptian captivity*

From Moses to Joshua

Toward the end of the 400 years, the people cried out to God for a deliverer. So God raised up a mighty deliverer named Moses. He told pharaoh God said, "Let my people go"! Pharaoh didn't listen so God sent plagues. They worshiped frogs so God gave them frogs! They worshiped the river so God turned the river into blood. All of the plagues were related to their gods. God brought about the plagues for three reasons: to convince Pharaoh to let the Israelites go, to convince the Israelites to follow Moses, and to put down the Egyptian gods. Moses led the nation of Israel out of Egypt. Then after parting the Red Sea, Moses led them south to Mt. Sinai, where God gave them the Law. At Mt. Sinai, Israel formally became a nation. God gave them the Law, which essentially became their constitution. The Law had three divisions: civil, ceremonial, and moral. The moral laws are called the 10 commandments, which are actually the first principles of the entire Law. There are 613 laws all together! God forms the entire law into a covenant with Israel: if they obey they will be blessed; if they disobey, they will be cursed. In many ways this forms the rest of the history of Israel, until the coming of Christ. They say they'll obey! So Moses leads them just south of the land promised to Abraham, to a city called Kadesh Barnea. They send 12 spies into the land, to see if they can take it. When the spies came back, 10 say no because they were afraid and 2 say let's go, God will give us victory. The two were Joshua and Caleb. As a result they decide not to enter the land, so God sentences them to wander in the wilderness for 40 years until everyone over 19 years old dies, everyone except Joshua and Caleb. Then Moses leads them up to the plains of Moab to enter the land a second time. Here he preaches five big sermons, in essence, a second giving of the Law before they go into the land: God promises again, if they obey the Law they will be blessed, and if they disobey they will be cursed. Moses dies and a new leader is raised up—Joshua.

Review

Then God raises up a deliverer: <u>Moses</u>
Pharaoh wouldn't let the Israelites go, so God brought about plagues for 3 reasons: <u>to convince Pharaoh, to convince Israel, and to put down the Egyptian gods.</u>
Moses then leads them out across what sea? <u>Red Sea</u>
They take a right to <u>Mt. Sinai</u>
where God gives them: <u>the Law</u>
The three divisions of the Law are: <u>civil, ceremonial, and moral</u>
The first principles of the Law are: <u>the 10 commandments</u>
How many laws are there all together? <u>613</u>
God makes a covenant with them—obey and be: <u>blessed</u>.
Disobey and be: <u>cursed</u>.
They say they will obey so Moses leads them across the wilderness to what town? <u>Kadesh Barnea</u>
Where they send how many spies into the land? <u>12</u>
And <u>10 say no and 2 say go</u>.
The two are: <u>Joshua and Caleb</u>
As a result they wander in the wilderness for how long? <u>40 years</u>
until: <u>everyone over 19 dies</u>
except: <u>Joshua and Caleb</u>
Moses then leads them up to: <u>the plains of Moab</u>
where he gives them the Law: <u>a second time</u>
Then God raises up a new leader, General: <u>Joshua</u>

From Joshua to the Exile

Joshua then leads them across the Jordan River at flood stage. Right square in their way, in the middle of Canaan, is in essence the capital of Canaan, <u>Jericho</u>. It had two huge walls around it, the inner wall was wide enough you could drive chariots on it. God gave them a strategy, which Joshua obeyed, to march around the walls each day for six days and on the seventh day to blow their horns and the walls would fall down. Archaeologists have uncovered those very walls today, one falling out and one falling in. We say they had a "<u>smashing success</u>." Next they went 14 miles NW to a much smaller city <u>Ai</u>, but they were defeated. Why? Because Achan stole some of the treasures and hid them in his tent, against God's command. We say they suffered "<u>Achan defeat</u>." Once Achan was taken care of, they won victories in the region of Gibeon by separating to the north and the south—an excellent military strategy. Then Joshua takes his soldiers on a Southern campaign, and they take the South <u>totally</u> as God commanded. He then turns North, but only takes the North <u>partially</u>, not fully obeying God. The land was then divided up into <u>12 parts</u> because of the twelve tribes of Israel—Jacob's 12 sons. Following the division of the land, God raises up judges to rule the land. Some judges were good and the people obeyed God, some were bad and the people disobeyed God. Some of the judges are well known: Deborah is the only female judge mentioned; we know Samson because of his great strength; and Gideon was a judge as well as a warrior. The period is characterized by ups and downs; we say it was characterized by anarchy. The people look around and see that everyone else has kings so they want a king. God tells them you don't want a king, he will tax you and you will have to serve him. Plus God did not want them to have a king, because He was their King, but the people insisted. So God gave them a king. God told Samuel, who was the last judge and the first prophet, to anoint the first king—Saul. After God removed Saul, God had Samuel anoint David as the second king, a man after God's own heart. God further clarified His promise, which He had made with Abraham, by promising David (in covenant form) that the coming king, who would bring in the kingdom, would come from David's line, establishing David's throne forever. So the third king was from his line: Solomon, David's son. He was the one who was to build a temple for God. David and Solomon wrote the heart of the Writings—the third section of the Jewish Scriptures; David wrote the Psalms, and Solomon wrote the wisdom literature: Proverbs, Ecclesiastes, and the Song of Solomon. The fourth king was Rehoboam, Solomon's son. He wanted to become richer than his father, so he taxed the people to death, and there was a revolt. The tribes split—10 go to the North and 2 go to the South. Jeroboam, a general, goes to the North and Rehoboam goes to the South. The 10 in the North are called Israel and the two in the South are called Judah.

Then God raises up prophets to try to shape up Israel and Judah, but no one listens. The writings of these prophets are in the section of the Prophets in the Jewish Scriptures called the Latter Prophets (Isaiah, Jeremiah, and Ezekiel and the Book of the 12 Minor Prophets). The Former Prophets give the history of the kings (1 and 2 Samuel and 1 and 2 Kings). Because they don't listen, what does God do? Just as He promised in His covenant with them at Mt. Sinai and in the second giving of the Law on the plains of Moab, He brings in the Assyrians from the North and takes the Northern tribes captive. This was 200 years after the split kingdom, in 722 BC. The Assyrians were cruel and feared for ripping their prisoners alive and displaying piles of human skulls. The prophets in the south then start prophesying to Judah but they don't listen. So God brings in the Babylonians who take them captive for 70 years, because they didn't let the land lay rest every seventh year as commanded in the Law, which was the plan to deal with the poor to let them start over. The Babylonians were educators, so they took young men like Daniel and his companions and educated them to serve the king by ruling over their own people. This was 150 years after the Assyrian captivity. Then a new empire takes over the Babylonians—the Medes and Persians (the history is recorded in the book of Daniel). Then God allows Judah to come back into the land in three expeditions. The first is led back by Zerubbabel, and he rebuilds the temple. The second is led back by Ezra, and he rebuilds the hearts of the people. The third is led back by Nehemiah, and he rebuilds the walls of the city of Jerusalem. Then there was a great silent period for 400 years between the Jewish Scriptures and the coming of Jesus the Messiah. The prominent world ruler during this time was Alexander the Great, and he was Greek, so the New Testament was written in Greek.

Review

Joshua leads them across what river? the <u>Jordan</u> to the "capital" city: <u>Jericho</u>, where they have <u>smashing success</u>.
They go 14 miles NW to a little town: <u>Ai</u> where they suffer: <u>Achan defeat</u>.
After they deal with Achan, they take the South how? <u>Totally</u>
And the North? <u>Partially</u>
Then they divide up the land into how many parts? <u>12</u>
Who are the prominent rulers during this time? <u>Judges</u>
Who was the female judge? <u>Deborah</u>
Who was the strong judge? <u>Samson</u>
Who was the judge "with all the Bibles"? <u>Gideon</u>
The period is characterized by: <u>anarchy</u>
Then they look around and see all the other nations have <u>kings</u>, so the last judge and the first prophet, who is also the king anointer: <u>Samuel</u>
Anoints the first king <u>Saul</u>, in the book of <u>1 Samuel.</u>
The second king is <u>David</u> in the book of <u>2 Samuel.</u>
God promised David his throne would last <u>forever</u>.
So the third king is <u>Solomon</u> Who is he? <u>David's son</u>; in the book of <u>1 Kings.</u>
The fourth king is <u>Rehoboam</u>. Who is he? <u>Solomon's son</u>
He wants to become richer than his father, so he taxes the people to death. As a result the kingdom splits.
Who goes to the North? <u>Jeroboam</u>
Who goes to the South? <u>Rehoboam</u>
How many tribes go North? <u>10</u>
How many tribes go South? <u>2</u>
The North is called? <u>Israel</u>
The South? <u>Judah</u>

Then God raises up prophets to try to shape up Israel and Judah, but no one listens. So who does God bring in from the North to take Israel captive? <u>The Assyrians</u>.
What kind of people are they? <u>Cruel</u>
How many years after the split kingdom? <u>200 years</u>
The prophets start going in the South, but nobody listens, so who does God bring in? <u>Babylonians</u> What kind of people are they? <u>Educators</u>
How long are they in captivity? <u>70 years</u>
Why? <u>Because they didn't let the land lay rest</u>
How many years is this captivity after the Assyrian captivity? <u>150 years</u>
Then a new empire takes over the Babylonians. Who are they? the <u>Medes and Persians.</u> They allow the Jews to come back in 3 expeditions:
The first is led back by <u>Zerubbabel</u> and he rebuilds the <u>temple</u>.
The second is led back by <u>Ezra</u> and he rebuilds their <u>hearts</u>.
The third is led back by <u>Nehemiah</u> and he rebuilds the <u>walls</u>.

> How long of a silent period between the completion of the Jewish Scriptures and the coming of Christ? <u>400 years</u>
> Who is the prominent world ruler during this time? <u>Alexander the Great</u>
> And he was a Greek so the New Testament is written in <u>Greek</u>.

Conclusion

All along as a nation, Israel missed the very purpose and plan God had for them. God wanted to bless all the families of the earth through them. Instead, they twisted the storyline. They completely misinterpreted the narrative of the Jewish Scriptures until Jesus came and shook up the whole law system they had twisted. Jesus had to open the minds of His followers to the accurate understanding of God's plan. In sessions 3–9 we will examine the key Scriptures and reset the Story, so we can accurately understand God's plan for mankind.

Read and Reflect on Key Quotes:

The quote in this session is from Walter Kaiser, who served as Old Testament dean at Trinity Evangelical Seminary and was president of Gordon Theological Seminary. As a young man in the 70s, seriously studying the Scriptures in our church context, I knocked on Walter Kaiser's door at Trinity and asked him to mentor me, because he had something I needed. He was, and is, considered the father of biblical theology (actually Old Testament theology) in the 20th century. He has served as a mentor to me ever since. This quote is from his book *The Promise-Plan of God: A Biblical Theology of the Old and New Testament*. We will also quote Kaiser extensively in upcoming sessions.

"In emphasizing the one unifying promise-plan of God as the theological center of the whole Bible rather than listing many random and scattered predictions (or even the absence of such an organizing mind behind revelation), this biblical theology differs from the task and results of the discipline known as *systematic theology*.

"Systematic theology has traditionally organized its approach around topics and themes such as God, humanity, sin, Christ, salvation, the church, and last things. By contrast, biblical theology has, more often than not, been a discipline in search of a mission and a structure—often falling into the same topical and structural tracks gone over by systematic theology, even though it severely criticized and stood aloof from systematic theology, claiming it had imposed an external grid (derived from philosophy or the like) on its material.

"Since its inception, biblical theology has had a strong diachronic strain that insists on tracing the historic development of doctrine as it appeared chronologically in the history of Israel and the church. Thus, while it had to be scriptural in *form* and *method* as well as in substance, it had to present itself in the order that God disclosed his revelation over the centuries or decades. It was to be a biblical theology, not a compilation of biblical *theologies* (on the alternative assumption that there was no unity or center to the canon).

The use of the singular noun in biblical theology implied that there was an organizing center that could be discovered—that the whole canon expressed the unity of the one mind and unified purpose of God. This unity had to be uncovered before exploring the plan and purpose of God as revealed in the individual books and sections of Scripture.

"The best proposal for such a unity is to be found exactly where Scripture itself pointed in its repeated references. I believe that the most suitable candidate for the unity or center of God's disclosure is to be found in the 'promise-plan' of God as revealed in repeated references throughout Scripture. The promise form of biblical theology focuses on one all-embracing divine word of promise rather than on its many scattered predictions (which is what most think of when they hear the word 'promise'), and it traces the growth of that declaration of God in the large teaching passages in each era of divine revelation. Usually in dogmatic or systematic theology, the texts used to support the doctrine discussed are scattered verses (rather than large 'chair,' or teaching chapters or pericopes) distributed over the length and breadth of the whole Bible.

"Whereas systematic theology generally separates prediction from promise, omitting references to the threatening aspect of the promise and the judgments of God as well as the historic *means* that God used to keep his word alive and ultimately to bring his word to pass, biblical theology insists on keeping both the threatening aspects and the predictions of hope together as alternative parts of the same promise-plan. It also traces the intermediate historic means, or links by which that word was maintained in partial fulfillments until the final and complete fulfillment came in Christ. Thus the promise was not simply a predictive word that remained inert and in word form only until it was finally fulfilled in its end point; it was a word that was maintained over the centuries in a continuing series of historic fulfillments that acted as earnests, or down payments on that word that still pointed to the last or final fulfillment."[2]

Record any insights from the brief commentary and quotes:

 ## Think Through the Issues

The nation of Israel completely and consistently rejected the unfolding plan of God and twisted the storyline. They missed the point of the Story.

ISSUE: Jesus' storyline—opening the minds of His followers

Think Through the Issue Before Discussion:

1. Even though they were God's chosen people, why do you think the nation of Israel missed the main point of the Story?
2. According to Jesus, what is the main point they missed?
3. What exactly did He explain to them?
4. Even though many of us know parts of the Story of Jesus, even those in other religions know them, why do you think we do not know the essence of the storyline today?

Record your initial thoughts on the issue before discussion:

Discuss the issue in your small group.

Record your initial thoughts on the issue after discussion:

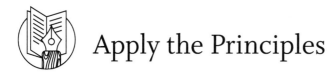# Apply the Principles

It is now time to respond to what you have studied and discussed. Take your time on this section.

Think Back Through the First Three Steps.

Design an Application for Your Life.

Whether we believe in Jesus or not or are a Christian or even if we are from another religion, we still need to understand this Story, since it is the storyline for Judaism, Christianity, and Islam, the only three world religions that combine history (the immanent) with the transcendent. (Hinduism, Buddhism, and Jainism, for example, recognize the spiritual but reject the "this world" historical realities.) After going through this session, summarize the essence of the big Story.

UNDERSTANDING THE SCRIPTURES 2

After His resurrection, when Jesus talked to His disciples on the road to Emmaus, Jesus opened the Scriptures to the two disciples. Beginning with Moses and all the Prophets, he "interpreted to them" all that had just happened. He was talking to men who thought they knew the Scriptures. But He essentially told them they had misunderstood the Scriptures. Later He appeared to all the disciples and opened their minds also. In fact, all of Israel had misunderstood the Scriptures. How could this happen? What did they misunderstand?

Most of us don't understand the Scriptures either. Just like Israel, most churches and Christians today don't understand the Scriptures. We don't have the Story right, and we don't have the framework Jesus referred to when He spoke of "the Law, the Prophets, and the Psalms."

So before we can understand what He explained to them, we must be introduced to the Scriptures: first to the Scriptures Jesus referred to on the road to Emmaus and then to the additional Scriptures written later by His disciples, the very disciples who up to that point had misunderstood them. Therefore, in this session, we will be introduced to the Scriptures. By the end of the ten sessions, we will understand what Jesus explained to them; and we will have a correct understanding of the Story.

Study the Scriptures

READ THE PASSAGES: LUKE 24:13–27, 44–49

Think Through the Questions:

1. What does the Luke passage tell us about the framework of the Scriptures?
2. What did the disciples understand about the Scriptures? What did they not understand?
3. What did Jesus clarify? What was His interpretation of the events of His death, burial, and resurrection?
4. What did it mean for Jesus to "open their minds" to understand? How do we know if Jesus was right?

Summarize the Core Teaching of the Passages:

Write a paragraph, outline, annotate, or chart your conclusions— whatever best communicates for you. Describe how Jesus viewed Himself and His own death, burial, and resurrection.

Core teaching of Luke 24:13–27, 44–49:

Consult the Scholars

The following comments are designed to help you better understand the passage and to stimulate your thinking on the implications of the teaching.

Read and Reflect on this Brief Commentary on Luke 24:13-27, 44-49

The Composite Apostolic Storyline: The Old Testament Walk Through, Part 2—The Old Testament Books

There are two ways of grasping the story. Bloom's educational taxonomy argues that the first two steps in the foundation of learning are necessary before you can apply what you are learning. The first is "remember." In our case, that would be when you actually can recall the core elements of the story. The second is when you begin to really understand the things you have memorized. In session one, we worked on just recalling the storyline. In this commentary, we will work towards understanding the storyline with a more detailed understanding of the Law, the Prophets, and the Writings, as the Scriptures were originally organized.

The following chart will ideally be taught by adding the Old Testament books to the Walk Through.

Grasping the Metanarrative in a Postmodern World

The Eleven Historical Books
(Tracing the chronology of the Old Testament)

The Law
1. Genesis—"the beginnings"
   - Genesis 12: beginning of walk through
   - Genesis 50: Joseph dies

2. Exodus—"the exodus"
   - Exodus 1: 400-year Egyptian captivity
   - Exodus 20: at Mt. Sinai getting the Law

3. Numbers—"the numberings"
   - Three events:
     1. a numbering of the people
     2. failure and wandering in the wilderness 40 years
     3. a second numbering in the plains of Moab

The Prophets
4. Joshua
   - First half of book: conquering the land
   - Second half of book: dividing the land

5. Judges
   - Period of spiritual ups and downs.
   - People disobeyed and were taken captive. Then God raised up a judge to deliver. When the judge died, people sinned and taken captive again.

6. 1 Samuel
   - Saul was the king.

7. 2 Samuel
   - David was the king.

8. 1 Kings
   - Solomon was the king. This also describes the split kingdom and a few kings in the north and east.

9. 2 Kings
   - Describes king of North and South and both the Assyrian and Babylonian captivities.

10. Ezra & Nehemiah (in The Writings)
    - Esther fits here—she was a queen, an instrument in allowing the Jews to come back from captivity. All three migrations back from the Babylonian captivity are described in Ezra and Nehemiah.

Additional Books Related to the Time Period of the Eleven Historical Books

Job—because of age of book

Leviticus—detailed book of the laws given at Mt. Sinai.

Deuteronomy—a second giving of the Law at plains of Moab before going into the land.

The Writings
No books parallel this period.

Ruth—these things took place in the days of the judges.

No books parallel this period.

Psalms—most of them.

Proverbs
Ecclesiastes
Song of Solomon

All the prophets except:

    Those during the Babylonian captivity: Ezekiel, Daniel.

    Those after the Babylonian captivity: Haggai, Zechariah, Malachi

Note: 1 & 2 Chronicles look at the same basic period as 1 & 2 Samuel and 1 & 2 Kings, only from a priestly instead of a political perspective.

See *How to Teach the Story* for an explanation on teaching this chart. First, the leader reviews the Walk Through, Part 1 from session one, with the group participating. Next, the leader walks the group back through the Walk Through, adding the books of the books where they fit chronologically with the Story. The leader asks the question "What book are we in in when God makes a promise to Abraham?" The leader explains each book of the chart, while standing in the right place on the map. He moves to the location of an event and asks, "What book are we in now?" Then the leader asks what other books go with this period, e.g. when David was king, "Did David write any books?" David wrote Psalms, so they fit there. If there is no leader, then the chart could be memorized, picturing the storyline location in the Walk Through.

The Road to Emmaus: Understanding the Scriptures—the Law, the Prophets, and the Writings

The story of Jesus on the road to Emmaus, after His resurrection, gives us the starting point for accurately understanding the Scriptures. Jesus went up to them and asked what they were discussing. The two disciples actually stated what needed to be explained from the Scriptures: Jesus of Nazareth was a prophet, mighty in word and deed, but was condemned to death and crucified; the one they thought was the promised Messiah who would redeem Israel was now missing from the grave on the third day. Thus they were in a state of confusion.

Jesus' explanation to the two disciples and to their companions later—all the key disciples—framed in the answer in Luke 24:25–27 and verses 44–49.

> [25] Then he said to them, "Oh, how foolish you are, and how slow of heart to believe all that the prophets have declared! [26] Was it not necessary that the Messiah should suffer these things and then enter into his glory?" [27] Then beginning with Moses and all the prophets, he interpreted to them the things about himself in all the scriptures.... [44] Then he said to them, "These are my words that I spoke to you while I was still with you—that everything written about me in the law of Moses, the prophets, and the psalms must be fulfilled." [45] Then he opened their minds to understand the scriptures, [46] and he said to them, "Thus it is written, that the Messiah is to suffer and to rise from the dead on the third day, [47] and that repentance and forgiveness of sins is to be proclaimed in his name to all nations, beginning from Jerusalem. [48] You are witnesses of these things. [49] And see, I am sending upon you what my Father promised; so stay here in the city until you have been clothed with power from on high."

The essence of Jesus' explanation was this: The Scriptures—the Law, the Prophets, and the Psalms—all pointed to Him and these events, which they did not understand correctly. The Messiah was to suffer, die, and rise again; and they were to repent and receive forgiveness of sins. This message was to be proclaimed by them, in His name, to all nations, beginning in Jerusalem.

Wow! That is a powerful statement: All the Scriptures point to Him. Everything. Then He gave them the right interpretation and opened their minds. And then, after they understood, they were to explain it to the whole world, in His name no less! That immediately raises some basic questions: How do we know what He said to them? Was He right? And how can we know for sure?

The only way we can know is to read the Scriptures ourselves. We must follow Jesus' explanation back through the Law, the Prophets, and the Psalms. But we don't have the details He used when He walked through the Scriptures with them. However, we can recreate it! After they understood, they were to proclaim this understanding—this "accurate interpretation"—to the whole world. A very useful little book was written in 1952 entitled *According to the Scriptures: The Sub-Structure of New Testament Theology* by C. H. Dodd, a Manchester, Oxford, and Cambridge scholar. He makes a powerful case that we can enter the basic conversation Jesus had with the two disciples on the road to Emmaus. How? Remember, Jesus told the disciples to proclaim His message, His interpretation of the Scriptures, to the whole world, beginning in Jerusalem. And that's what they did! We have the story of them doing that in Acts. Then we have their letters and the Gospels they wrote, which became additional Scriptures, what we call the *New Testament*. We can see how they backed up Jesus' interpretation—His proof of Himself—in the Law, the Prophets, and the Psalms. We can see for ourselves, from their lips, the essence of His interpretation—His proofs. While we won't follow all the same examples as Dodd, we will follow the method and study the Scriptures ourselves in sessions 3–9. We will study the Scriptures focused on in Peter's sermons in Acts and the additional "key passages" focused on by the disciples (which we will call the Apostles of Jesus) and their companions in the letters and the Gospels they wrote.

Here is the list of Scriptures we will study:

The Storyline: The Overall Plan
   Key text: Genesis 12:1–3
   Corollary texts: Genesis 15:1–6; 17:1–8

The Storyline: The Nation of Israel
   Key text: Exodus 19:1–6
   Corollary texts: Exodus 20:1–17; Deuteronomy 30:1–10; 18:15–22

The Storyline: The Coming Kingdom
   Key text: 2 Samuel 7:1–29
   Corollary texts: Psalms 89:1–4, 30–37; 16:8–11; 110:1–6; Isaiah 9:1–7

The Storyline: The Kingdom Arrives
   Key text: Mark 1:1–15
   Corollary texts: Mark 8:27–31; 9:30–32; 10:32–34; 12:35–37; 14:22–25; 16:14–18; Acts 10:34–43; 1 Corinthians 15:1–6
   Old Testament validation texts: Isaiah 53:1–12 (Songs of the Servant)

The Storyline: The Kingdom Launched
  Key text: Acts 1:1–8 (plus 6 summary verses)
  Corollary texts: Luke 1:1–4; 24:44–48; Acts 2:37–42; 8:1–5; 11:19–26; 13:1–14:28
  Old Testament validation texts: Isaiah 49:5–6; Genesis 12:1–3

The Storyline: The Church
  Key text: Ephesians 2:11–3:13; 4:1–16
  Corollary texts: Matthew 16:13–20; Acts 2:42–47; 1 Peter 2:1–10
  Old Testament validation texts: Isaiah 28:16; Psalm 118:22–23

The Storyline: The Kingdom Fully Realized
  Key text: Matthew 23:37–24:31
  Corollary texts: Acts 1:1–11; Romans 9:1–8, 30–33; 10:1–4; 11:25–27
  Old Testament validation texts: Zechariah 14:1–9

We studied the basic storyline in session one—the history of the Law, the Prophets, and the Psalms. In this session, we will study the framework of the Old Testament Scriptures—the Law, the Prophets, and the Writings, which we call *the Old Testament*. Then we need to understand the writings of the Apostles—the letters, Acts, and the Gospels—which we call *the New Testament*. At the time of Jesus, the basic formation of the Scriptures was the Law, the Prophets and the Psalms.

The Law: The five books of Moses (Genesis, Exodus, Leviticus, Numbers, and Deuteronomy), the first five books of the Old Testament.

The Prophets: There are two divisions—the former prophets and the latter prophets. They tell the history of Israel from a theological perspective.

  The Former Prophets: The main history of Israel and her kings (1 and 2 Samuel and 1 & 2 Kings)

  The Latter Prophets: The major prophets (Ezekiel, Isaiah, and Jeremiah) and the minor prophets (the Book of the 12), both continue the history of Israel, but warn of the judgment of the nation because of their disobedience to the law of Moses.

The Writings: The Writings are often referred to as the Psalms because Psalms is the first and the largest book of the collrction of the Writings. (The Writings include 150 Psalms in five books, small books like novellas, and various poetic forms).

Let's look at them in a little more depth along with the Scripture written by Jesus' Apostles and their companions, which we call the New Testament. The following is a summary of the whole story or purpose of the Bible (the canon of the faith—the "rule of faith") and shows how the books of the Bible contribute to that story.

The Scriptures

God's central plan, His eternal purpose, in which He sets apart for Himself a people, for all eternity, commissioning them to be witnesses of His purpose and supplying them with a book that contains all the essential insights and guidance they need to effectively assist Him in carrying out His purpose, which demonstrates His wisdom to the rulers and authorities in heavenly places.

The Scriptures Before Christ (Old Testament—The Law, The Prophets, and the Writings)

The Law

The Law set the stage for revealing His plan—It narrates the creation and fall of man; gives a glimmer of a promise of restoration, embedded in the curse to the woman and traced from Adam to Abraham; and gives insight into the major themes necessary to live in harmony with God's created order and to understand man's tendency to resist that order. (Gen. 1–11)

The Law revealed the promise to bless all the families of the earth through Abraham and his descendants—sovereignly forming those descendants into a nation through which God would reveal Himself and His plan to all the other nations; contracting with that nation concerning how they should live;

> as well as giving insight into living by faith in the plan of God and man's tendency to resist that plan and go his own way. (Genesis 12–50, Exodus, Leviticus, Numbers, Deuteronomy)

The Prophets

The prophets record the history of the nation of Israel, through whom God continued to sovereignly unfold His plan; and, in His covenant with David, He revealed an additional aspect of His promise to bless all the families of the earth— looking forward to a coming descendant of David who would rule forever,

> continuing to give insight into living by faith in the plan of God, again emphasizing and illustrating man's tendency to resist that plan and go his own way. (Joshua, Judges, 1 & 2 Samuel, 1 & 2 Kings)

The Prophets also record the prophetic word of the prophets who called Israel to court for her constant disobedience to the Law (Mosaic) Covenant, announcing impending judgment, while providing an ever broadening picture of the coming Messiah and the New Covenant, which would replace the Old (Mosaic) Covenant and would lead to all the promises made to Israel being fulfilled,

> giving the people of God insight into the true condition of their hearts and exhortations to proper repentance and godly morality. (Isaiah through Malachi)

The Writings (or "The Psalms")

The Writings preserved the psalms of David and those who wrote in his tradition, providing the people of God with a sort of "theological hymnbook" for worship and reflection, both individually and corporately,

> that they might internalize the Scriptures, up through the era of David and continuing to the time after they were exiled, that they might acquire hearts for God. (Psalms)

The Writings also include several small books like novellas of the stories of people God used in the Story; the wisdom literature of king Solomon; the majestic, civilization-wide prophecies of Daniel; and a theological history of the Prophets in 1 and 2 Chronicles.

The Scriptures After Christ (Paul's Letters, Peter's Letters, the Gospels, and John's Writings)

Paul's Letters (also Acts written by Luke, Paul's companion)

Acts is a catechetical narrative recording the actions of the Apostles, especially Paul, that focuses on the birth and expansion of Christ's new covenant community, His Church, which unfolded as the worldwide multiplication of churches—God's plan for carrying out Jesus' commission of being witnesses, beginning in Jerusalem.

Paul's letters establish the churches in the gospel and reveal in detail Christ's plan for the building and functioning of His Church—a design that when followed would ultimately cause the rulers and authorities in heavenly places to recognize the manifold wisdom of God.

The Jewish Letters

These letters, written by Peter and other Jewish church leaders to Jewish churches scattered everywhere, were designed to keep them from returning to Judaism, since the Apostles were growing old and a new generation of leaders was emerging,

> with a view of fully integrating them into the Church, as it gradually became clear to them that the Church was God's plan to unfold the kingdom, replacing Israel, which was facing impending judgment.

The Gospels (Mark, Matthew, Luke, John)

The Gospels record and interpret, in narrative form, the life and ministry of Christ, in which Jesus and His offer of the kingdom was rejected and a new phase in the plan of God was revealed, that is His Church, a new community, which Christ gathered together and began building, over which no force, not even the gates of Hades, would be able to prevail, with particular focus on fully establishing the churches in the good news of Jesus and inaugurating His kingdom, keeping them strong in the faith so they wouldn't leave the faith, since the Apostles were soon to leave the scene.

John's Letters and Revelation

These letters were written by John to his network of seven churches, challenging them to remain in the faith, with a body of teaching (theology) of loving one another while remaining in the truth,

climaxing with the recording of Jesus' apocalyptic visions given to John, containing the ultimate fulfillment of the whole plan of God, designed to help the seven churches (and all future churches) evaluate themselves in order to remain strong for the coming battles as the kingdom unfolded, finishing with the unfolding of the civilization-wide prophecies of Daniel.

That is the context of understanding the Scriptures Jesus used, as well as the Scriptures written by His Apostles and companions after His ascension to heaven. In session three, we will enter the Emmaus road conversation with Jesus.

Read and Reflect on Key Quotes:

The first quote we want to look at in this session is from James D. G. Dunn. He is Lightfoot Professor Emeritus of Divinity at the University of Durham, England. He has written the most exhaustive work to date on the quest for the historical church in the early Graeco-Roman world. It is found in volumes 2 and 3 of his mammoth 3-volume work, *Christianity in the Making* (Eerdmans, completed November 2015). This quote, based on Dodd's work, is from an earlier volume in 1977.

"One of the most important and unifying factors in Christianity has been mutual recognition in certain writings as foundational and normative, or, in a word, as scripture. Moreover, those who have vigorously contested the role of tradition have done so in defense of the primary and unequalled authority of the Bible. Was the same true of the earliest churches' Bible? The only Bible they knew and recognized were the Jewish scriptures, that is the Law and the Prophets, together with other Writings whose authority and whose number were not yet fully agreed, but which coincided more or less with what Christians call 'the Old Testament.' We shall use this last term (OT) for convenience. But we must recognize that in the first century AD it is both too precise and an anachronism, since *Old Testament* presupposes that there is already a *New* Testament, which of course did not yet exist as such.

"We need to spend a little time demonstrating that *the OT is an important unifying element in earliest Christianity and in the earliest Christian literature*. This is obviously true in the more specifically Jewish Christian writings: notice the frequent use of the phrase 'in order that it might be fulfilled' in Matthew and John and the important role played by scriptural quotation in the early speeches in Acts, in Rom. 9–11 and in Hebrews. But it is also true throughout the NT. A glance at a Nestle Greek text shows on almost every page words in different type, denoting a direct scriptural reference (the Johannine epistles are a striking exception)—and that does not include the less clear-cut allusions. In this sense all Christianity in the NT is Jewish Christianity; that is to say, the influence of the OT pervades the whole, determines the meaning of its categories and concepts.

"C. H. Dodd made much the same point in his significant book, *According to the Scriptures*, by subtitling it *The Sub-structure of New Testament Theology*:

> The whole body of material—the passages of OT scriptures with their application to the gospel facts—is common to all the main portions of the NT, and in particular it provided *the starting point for the theological constructions* of Paul, the author to the Hebrews, and the Fourth Evangelist. *It is the substructure of all Christian theology and contains already its chief regulative ideas.*

"This is a bold claim. If it is true then we have indeed a unifying element of primary significance, perhaps as important a unifying factor as faith in Jesus itself—not just 'gospel facts' but 'OT scripture,' not just Jesus but OT. So far we have seen that in kerygma, in confession and in tradition, Jesus alone gives unity and coherence to the diversity of formulations. Do we now have to add another block to the foundation of Christianity—the OT? Is the real basis of early Christian unity Jesus *and* the OT?

"The relation between NT and OT, and vice-versa, is one which has fascinated scholars for centuries, and the mass of literature which has appeared in recent years indicates that the debate has been particularly lively over the past two decades. Fortunately the concerns of the present study enable us both to narrow the question down and to sharpen it as well. For the key question is not so much whether the Jewish scriptures were authoritative, as *how their authority was understood in practice*. The same is true of the modern debate about biblical authority: what is the Bible's authority when the meaning of a text cannot be fully determined but has to be left ambiguous? What is the Bible's authority when on the same topic one author says one thing and another something else? We have already seen a fair amount of that kind of diversity in the last three chapters, and the diversity of denominations within Christianity is living testimony to the diversity of interpretation possible in biblical exegesis. The key question for us then is not whether the OT was regarded as authoritative, but what was its authority in practice? How were the Jewish scriptures actually handled in the first years of Christianity? How did the first Christians actually use the OT?"[3]

The following quote is from C. H. Dodd, an Oxford graduate who spent his career at Oxford. In his body of work, he dusted off and resurrected the concepts of *the kerygma* and *the didache*, which are the substructure of New Testament theology. His work built on *Testimonies*, by J. Rendel Harris (Cambridge, 2012), also a professor at Manchester. These two works, along with Dunn, represent just over a 100 year-conversation and research rediscovering the kerygma and the didache as the foundation of the New Testament theology of the Early Church.

"THE historical study of New Testament theology, as distinct from dogmatic or systematic theology, is faced by the difficult task of discovering the true starting-point of the development which the New Testament writings exhibit. It seems that the soundest method towards that end is to isolate, among the rich variety of these writings, those elements which are so widely common to them that they must be regarded as forming part of a central tradition, by which they were all more or less controlled. It should then be possible to arrive at some probable estimate of the extent to which this common tradition is primitive, or at least capable of being traced back to as early a period in the history of the Church as our research can reasonably expect to reach. This would give us, not necessarily, or not only, a theoretical basis for doctrine, but a genuinely chronological starting point for the history of Christian thought.

"It may fairly be said that a considerable degree of consent has now been achieved about the character and contents of the common and central tradition. It appears to have at its core what the New Testament itself calls the *kerygma*, or proclamation of the Gospel. In its most summary form the *kerygma* consists of the announcement of certain historical events in a setting which displays the significance of those events. The events in question are those of the appearance of Jesus in history—His ministry, sufferings and death and His subsequent manifestation of Himself to His followers as risen from the dead and invested with the glory of another world—and the emergence of the Church as a society distinguished by the power and activity of the Holy Spirit, and looking forward to the return of its Lord as Judge and Saviour of the world.

"The significance attached to these events is mainly indicated by references to the Old Testament. In the few clauses of the *kerygma* which are preserved in I Cor. xv. 3–5 it is said that Christ died, and rose the third day, 'according to the scriptures.' In the more formal summary outlines of the *kerygma* which are given in Acts it is a constant theme that in the coming of Christ, His death and resurrection, the prophecies are fulfilled....

"In various parts of the New Testament, notably in the Epistles of Paul, the Epistle to the Hebrews, and the Gospel and Epistles of John, we have a theological edifice constructed upon this plan. The style of building differs considerably. The theology of Paul, of John, and of the author to the Hebrews, though based upon a common tradition of the centre, is far from uniform. As church architecture, based upon a universal general plan, may show the various characteristics of Romanesque, Gothic or Baroque, so each of these theologians builds after his own style. It is a great merit of modern critical study of the New Testament that it has made us appreciate the individuality of the great theologians of the apostolic age, and the rich diversity of their teaching. The question now before us is this: Granted that each of these early thinkers followed the general tradition embodied in the apostolic *kerygma*, and faithfully conserved its main outline, have they anything in common beyond the bare outline? To put it otherwise, given the ground-plan, and the majestic buildings erected to its pattern, can we find a substructure—a part of the actual edifice—which is common to them all, or are the several buildings individually different from the foundation up?"⁴

The final quote in this session is again from Walter Kaiser. We will look at a quote from his work *Recovering the Unity of the Bible: One Continuous Story, Plan, and Purpose*. Then in sessions 3–6, we will revisit this book and use four excerpts of one long, continuous quote.

"Jewish tradition divided the Hebrew Bible into three parts identified by the acronym TaNaK, in which the first division was designated by *T* for the Torah or Law (Genesis, Exodus, Leviticus, Numbers, and Deuteronomy); the second division was denoted by *N* for *Nebi'im*, the Prophets, both the Former Prophets (Joshua, Judges, Samuel, and Kings; the last two books were taken as one book each despite our English division of the books into 1 and 2 Samuel and 1 and 2 Kings) and the Latter Prophets (Isaiah, Jeremiah, Ezekiel, and the twelve Minor Prophets, which were all taken as one book); and the third division was marked by *K* for *Ketubim*, the Writings, which in turn were made up of the three poetical books (Psalms, Proverbs, and Job), the five Megillot, or Scrolls (Song of Songs, Ruth, Lamentations, Ecclesiastes, and Esther), and the Histories (Daniel, Ezra-Nehemiah, 1 and 2 Chronicles). (The two *a* vowels in TaNaK were supplied between the *T*, the *N*, and the *K* to help pronounce the acronym.)

"Freedman noted the following distributions and proportions of these major divisions of the Hebrew Bible, consisting of 305,500 words in the Hebrew Bible, rounded off to 300,000:

Torah/Law	5 books	80,000 words	Primary History
Former Prophets	4 books	70,000 words	Primary History
Latter Prophets	4 books	72,000 words	
Writings	11 books	84,000 words	

"What he labeled the 'core Bible' of the Old Testament, or the 'Primary History,' comprises about 150,000 words, or one-half of the entire Hebrew Bible. In these nine books, the central content of the Bible can be found. From this perspective, the center or apex of the Hebrew Bible comes at the end of the Primary History—the point at which the story is told of the Babylonian captivity of the people of Judah, the loss of Israel's nationhood, and the complete destruction of the capital of Judah, Jerusalem."⁵

Record any insights from the brief commentary and quotes:

Think Through the Issues

Jesus opened the minds of the two disciples on the road to Emmaus because they had missed the point of the Story. They knew the Scriptures but did not understand them correctly. According to Jesus' core explanation, most Jewish people still do not understand the Scriptures because they don't accept Jesus as the Messiah. They don't accept His explanation of who He was and what He did. The Jews were the heart of the Story of the Scriptures up to that point, but they interpreted the Scriptures incorrectly. Most churches today call the Jewish Scriptures the Old Testament and possess the New Testament, which contains the rest of the Story, but they misunderstand the rest of the Story; in fact, most Christians misunderstand the whole Story.

As we study this booklet, we need to reflect on the implications of studying the Bible without an accurate understanding of the Story. It is possible, in fact highly likely, that even though we have access to all the Scriptures now and most own a Bible, we do not know what we possess. That is why we are now in a post-Christian culture in the West. It is critical that we have an accurate understanding of the Scriptures. We will now reflect on that and what it will take to understand the Scriptures accurately.

ISSUE: Understanding the Scriptures

Think Through the Issue Before Discussion:

1. How can you explain the fact that most Jewish people and most churches do not understand the Scriptures?
2. How can we know that we have an accurate understanding?
3. How do we know if Jesus was right in His understanding?
4. What is involved in having our minds opened up to an accurate understanding?
5. What does that process look like? What kind of commitment is needed on our part to assure we are interpreting things correctly?

> Record your initial thoughts on the issue before discussion:

Discuss the issue in your small group.

Record your initial thoughts on the issue after discussion:

Apply the Principles

It is now time to respond to what you have studied and discussed. Take your time on this section.

Think Back Through the First Three Steps.

Design an Application for Your Life.

Write you own summary of what you have learned from this study in Luke about the essence of understanding the Scriptures. Write a prayer asking God to open up your mind to understanding the Scriptures. Record your commitment to this 10-week process.

THE OVERALL PLAN ③

As we have been discussing, shortly after His resurrection, Jesus was walking on the road to Emmaus with two of His disciples, and He opened their minds to understand the Scriptures. He put the whole picture together. After He left the scene, it was the job of His followers to begin the process of both understanding and communicating to others how Jesus fulfilled the Scriptures—the Law, the Prophets, and the Writings. In Acts we have Peter's five sermons, which we call the *keryma*—the proclamation of Jesus, the Story of what had happened. In his second sermon, Acts 3:11–25, Peter begins by referring to "the God of Abraham, Isaac, and Jacob," the God of our fathers, as having glorified Jesus. He ends with a reference from Genesis 12:1–3 in which he refers to a covenant God made with Abraham.

In Acts 7, just before he was stoned, Stephen gave a sermon in story form surveying the storyline of the Scriptures (in the tradition of Jesus on the road to Emmaus). He began with a quote from Genesis 12:1–3. Why is that passage so important? Why would they begin at that point in telling the Story of Jesus and not at the beginning of Genesis? In this session, we too will begin examining the Story of Jesus in the context of the story of Israel, which we will see provides the storyline of the Scriptures.

Study the Scriptures

READ THE PASSAGES: GENESIS 12:1–3; 15:1–6; 17:1–8

Think Through the Questions:

1. Why do you think Genesis 12:1–3 is so important?
2. Why would both Peter and Stephen choose to begin with that passage to explain the Story of Jesus from the Scriptures?
3. In what way does this passage set the stage for the metanarrative (the big Story) of the Scriptures?
4. What are the basic elements of the overall plan laid out there?

Summarize the Core Teaching of the Passages:

Summarize the story behind these three passages, and comment on why Genesis 12:1–3 is so important in understanding the storyline of the Scriptures—the Law, the Prophets, and the Writings. Try to identify the skeleton of the plan that is set in motion here, which will eventually include all the nations of the earth.

Core teaching of Genesis 12:1–3; 15:1–6; 17:1–8:

 # Consult the Scholars

The following comments are designed to help you better understand the passage and to stimulate your thinking on the implications of the teaching.

Read and Reflect on This Brief Commentary on Genesis 12:1–3; 15:1–6; and 17:1–8.

When the two disciples went back to join the other disciples and followers, as recorded later in Luke 24, Jesus appeared in their midst and opened their minds to the Scriptures, the same way He had done for them. After Jesus left, they began proclaiming to others the things that had happened around them and Jesus' claim of inaugurating the kingdom. They explained to others how the Scriptures pointed to all of this, quoting from the Scriptures in their sermons and writings.

C. H. Dodd, a Cambridge professor and theologian in the mid 20th century, catalogued the Scripture quotes they used the most to validate the Story of Jesus. A list of "testimonies" from the Scriptures are listed in Appendix B of this booklet—"The Story: Testimonies." We will study the core of these passages in this booklet. These first and foundational quotes are built from Genesis 12–15, the focus being Genesis 12:1–3, with two corollary passages: Genesis 15:1–6 and 17:1–8. Let's turn to these now.

Genesis 12:1–3

Our Story begins with Abram and several promises God made to him. Who was Abram? Abram was in the line of descendants of Noah. After Adam and Eve sinned and were thrown out of the garden of Eden, from their children, "men began to multiply across the earth," but they became evil and rejected God. Only Noah found favor with God and was preserved in the ark as God destroyed man through a worldwide flood. After the flood, Noah's children also multiplied across the earth, forming nations, but again they rejected God, as was illustrated in the story of the Tower of Babel. There the nations gathered together and built a city and tower as a symbol of replacing God with man's kingdom. As a result, God scattered them and broke up their common language. The ancestral lines of Noah's three sons are recorded. Abraham was from the line of Shem, one of Noah's three sons.

As we learned in the first session of this booklet, "The Storyline," Abram had a wife Sarah and a nephew Lot. His father was Terah. Abram, left Ur of the Chaldeans with Sarah, Terah, and Lot in order to enter Canaan, and they traveled as far as Haran, where Terah died. At this point, God directly enters the scene.

The section in 12:1 simply begins with "Now the Lord said to Abram . . . ."

> 12:1 Now the LORD said to Abram, "Go from your country and your kindred and your father's house to the land that I will show you. ² I will make of you a great nation, and I will bless you, and make your name great, so that you will be a blessing. ³ I will bless those who bless you, and the one who curses you I will curse; and in you all the families of the earth shall be blessed."

Here God promises Abram three things:
1. Land
2. Descendants—a great nation
3. Blessing

The key here is in the last line: "in you all the families of the earth shall be blessed." In the context of Genesis up to this point, that means all the nations of the earth. Until now, man has completely failed and the nations have rejected God. But through Abram and the nation God would grow from his family, God would bless them, and that nation would bring blessing to all the nations of the earth. That is quite a promise.

Let's go on with the narrative. God marks out the specific land He has in mind (Genesis 12:4–9). It is basically the nation of Israel today. Abram became very rich and eventually separated from Lot. Now Abram has done all that God asked: He left his country and his father's house and his relatives. God reaffirms that he will have this land forever.

Genesis 15:1–6, 18–21

In this passage, God revisits the promise He made to Abram, reaffirming His commitment to give him descendants. Then a new piece of the promise becomes clear: the first descendant, who would multiply into a great nation, would come from his own body, 15:4–5. Abram's response is very important at this point in 15:6.

> "Then he believed in the Lord; and he reckoned it to him as righteousness."

We will see that this verse became part of the Apostles' validation of the Story that the Scriptures point to Jesus. But for now, we can see that Abram was counted as righteous by God, not because of his good deeds or works, but because of his faith. He believed in the promise of God to bring about a nation from him that would bless all the families of the earth. The development of the promise gets more specific with the connection of the descendants to the land at the end of the chapter, 15:18–21.

> "[18] On that day the LORD made a covenant with Abram, saying, "To your descendants I give this land, from the river of Egypt to the great river, the river Euphrates, [19] the land of the Kenites, the Kenizzites, the Kadmonites, [20] the Hittites, the Perizzites, the Rephaim, [21] the Amorites, the Canaanites, the Girgashites, and the Jebusites."

So God makes it into a formal covenant with Abram.

Genesis 17:1–8

Now the whole picture becomes clear, after a fiasco of Sarah trying to help God along. Since she was barren, she suggested to her husband to have a child through her handmaid Hagar, which gave birth to a son Ishmael. God stepped in and promised to establish His covenant with Abram, and at 99, He gave him a son through Sarah, named Isaac. Here is the full development of the promise that was given in 12:1–3.

> 17:1 When Abram was ninety-nine years old, the LORD appeared to Abram, and said to him, "I am God Almighty; walk before me, and be blameless. [2] And I will make my covenant between me and you, and will make you exceedingly numerous." [3] Then Abram fell on his face; and God said to him, [4] "As for me, this is my covenant with you: You shall be the ancestor of a multitude of nations. [5] No longer shall your name be Abram, but your name shall be Abraham; for I have made you the ancestor of a multitude of nations. [6] I will make you exceedingly fruitful; and I will make nations of you, and kings shall come from you. [7] I will establish my covenant between me and you, and your offspring after you throughout their generations, for an everlasting covenant, to be God to you and to your offspring after you. [8] And I will

give to you, and to your offspring after you, the land where you are now an alien, all the land of Canaan, for a perpetual holding; and I will be their God."

It is clear that Abraham will be the father of a nation through whom God will bless all the families (nations) of the earth. Thus through becoming the father of a great nation, Abraham will become the father of a multitude of nations. And we can see that this is an everlasting covenant.

Now let's put the entire picture together—essentially a promise that is also a plan which shapes all future history of the nations of the world. We know very little about how all this will happen at this point in the Story, but we have the essential framework for the metanarrative of history put in place.

The Plan for the History of Mankind (metanarrative)

1. God chose one man and his family to build a nation that would eventually bless all the nations of the world.
2. He specifically made a covenant with that man, Abraham, that He would bring about the fulfillment of the promise, which would solve the problem of the nations continually rejecting God (as seen in Genesis 1–11).
3. This nation would be based in the land of Canaan (from the river of Egypt to the Euphrates) and would increase from his own ancestral line—through Isaac.
4. Abraham's own righteousness was based on faith in this promise, not on some personal righteousness attained by his own efforts.

So here we have the foundation of the metanarrative—the framework of a grand story. We do not know the details yet, but we do know that the disciples (the Apostles) saw this as the starting point of the Story as it was revealed to them by Jesus, as He opened their minds to understand the Scriptures. How will we know if it is true? As it unfolds, we should expect to find several things to be true: It should match history unfolding around us today; it should unfold as one cohesive story; it should validate the events around the life, death, burial, and resurrection of Christ; and it should be consistent with the plan Christ revealed. The next few sessions will tell the tale.

Read and Reflect on Key Quotes:

Though Walter Kaiser was Old Testament dean at Trinity Evangelical Seminary, president of Gordon Theological Seminary, and considered to be the father of Old Testament theology, he makes his ideas accessible in his book *Recovering the Unity of the Bible: One Continuous Story, Plan, and Purpose*. I have chosen a long quote from this book, which traces the Story in some of the main historic epochs of biblical history; we will look at excerpts of this quote in sessions 3–6 of this booklet. In this session we will look at the time of the patriarchs.

"If the formal announcement of God's plan began with Abraham, then the ways in which it branched out and was fulfilled with an enlarged agenda and with other technical terms must be traced as it leads us into the New Testament. We will now follow it in several of the main historic epochs of biblical history.

"**The time of the patriarchs.** In the history of Israel as recorded in the Old Testament, the call of Abram along with the promise provisions is singled out as the principal theme. It actually consists of a number of subordinate things and then of a more principal item.

"There are, according to some counts, some seven subordinate items promised to Abraham, Isaac, and Jacob. They include: (1) 'seed,' that is, a posterity with a large number of descendants (Gen. 13:16; 15:5, 15–16; 26:4; 28:3–4; 35:11–12; 48:3–4); (2) a posterity that would become a 'great nation' (Gen. 18:18; 35:11; 46:3); (3) descendants that would be or include 'an assembly/community of nations' (Gen. 17:6, 16; 28:3; 35:11; 48:4); (4) 'kings' who would arise from Abraham, Sarah, and Jacob (Gen. 17:6, 16; 35:11); (5) a posterity that would inherit the land of Canaan; (6) the possession of a 'great name' (Gen. 12:2–3); and (7) a posterity that would 'take possession of the cities of their enemies' (Gen. 22:17) in Canaan.

"However, none of these features amounted to the principal item. The emphasis fell, instead, on that part of the 'seed' that went all the way back to the *protoevangelium* in Genesis 3:15, where a male descendant from Eve's line would crush the head of 'the serpent.' But that was not all: through Abraham and that seed, 'all the nations of the earth would be blessed.' The passive form of the verb assured all that it would be God who would effect this, and not Abraham or his descendants. We can be sure that 'the blessing of all the nations' was where the emphasis of this promise fell, for this aspect of the promise was repeated five times in Genesis (12:3; 18:18; 22:18; 26:4; 28:14), always in the climactic or culminating position in the list of promises.

"Of special interest was the portion of the promise that referred to the 'seed.' Seed was not a plural word; instead, it was a collective noun. That is the way the apostle Paul read it as well. In Galatians 3:16, 19 Paul viewed the 'Seed as one that expressed a corporate solidarity, and one that had its culmination in none other than Jesus the Messiah.

"The promises were spoken to Abraham and to his seed. The Scripture does not say 'and to his seeds,' meaning many people, but 'and to your seed,' meaning one person, who is Christ: 'What, then, was the purpose of the law? It was added because of transgressions until the Seed to whom the promise referred had come' (Gal. 3:19).

"God's covenant with Abraham was based on the promise with special reference to the Seed. It was God who initiated and who took all the responsibility for maintaining this covenant (Gen. 15:1–6).

"One may question how far men like the patriarchs could have foreseen the future or understood what it was that was being promised to them. This much must have been clear to them: they and their descendants were being called eternally to be Yahweh's own people. Yahweh would be their God (Gen. 17:7–8; 28:21), and later he would add to this formula the two other parts—they would be his people, and he would come to dwell in the midst of them. In that they were told that the covenant was eternal (Gen. 17), they could expect that some of the events included in it would still be in progress beyond their times, even if they could not see as yet a person like Jesus arising to fulfill the heart of this promise. But they would also find the promise to be a religious doctrine that would hold the same place in their theology as the doctrine of Christ holds in our theology today. Therefore, they had certain things to believe, teach, and live out in everyday practice. In this way the promise was more than a prediction; it was a doctrine, and God's people were expected to believe and live according to it."[6]

Record any insights from the brief commentary and quotes:

Think Through the Issues

We now live in a postmodern society in which there is no longer a belief in a historical *metanarrative*—one big story that puts all of life and history together and explains its meaning and purpose. The Bible claims to be such a story. In this section, we have seen the foundation of this Story: that God inaugurated a plan through Abraham and his descendants that would eventually lead to all the families of the earth being blessed—happy and prosperous. As this Story unfolds in the following sessions over the next few weeks, it is important to determine whether this Story is true or not. This study is the first step in that process.

In this section, we will begin to reflect on whether to believe this Story or not. If it is true, then it will lead to understanding the purpose and meaning of all of history and of life itself, for that matter. It is the most important investment of time you can make, if you are not a believer in the Story. And if you are a believer in a different story, you will need to hold this Story up against it.

ISSUE: Framing the postmodern narrative

Think Through the Issue Before Discussion:

1. Do you find yourself attracted to the foundation of this Story, as you studied it in this session? Why are you attracted to it?
2. What will ultimately be your measure for whether you can conclude the Story is true?
3. If it turns out to be true, what are some of the foundational things you are called on to believe from these passages? What seems to be the overall plan?
4. In what ways are the truths in these passages unique to what you currently believe? What would change in your present worldview if you accepted the ideas of these Genesis passages?

Record your initial thoughts on the issue before discussion:

Discuss the issue in your small group.

Record your initial thoughts on the issue after discussion:

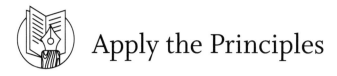 Apply the Principles

It is now time to respond to what you have studied and discussed. Take your time on this section.

Think Back Through the First Three Steps.

Design an Application for Your Life.

In this session, we have examined the foundations of the overall plan of God as described in Genesis 12–15, with a focus on Genesis 12:1–3. Record what would change in your overall view of life and history and ultimately your purpose and view of life, if you truly believe in this Story.

> Identify the main things that would change in your view of life and the world if you believe in this Story.

THE NATION OF ISRAEL ❹

The nation of Israel is a story within the Story. Again, we need to return to the Apostles to see what Old Testament passages they used to explain their understanding of the Story. In Peter's second sermon, Acts 3:11–26, we see important Bible stories unified in the same sermon. Peter quotes from both Genesis 12:1–3 (Abraham and God's covenant with him) and passages regarding Moses and God's covenant with him. In the covenant with Abraham, we see that all the families of the earth will be blessed through the nation that will come from his line. In the covenant with Moses and the nation Israel, we see the Story continue. The nation will be a "priestly nation" to all the nations. Peter goes back into a passage that the nation should listen to. In the context of the second giving of the law to the nation was a prediction that the nation itself would fail. In the context of Peter's sermon, this new prophet Jesus is seen as the one who will bring in that priestly kingdom. In this section, we will look at that covenant with Israel, the prediction of their coming failure, and again validate the storyline as it was unfolding after the death and resurrection of Christ.

Study the Scriptures

READ THE PASSAGES: EXODUS 19:1–6; 20:1–17; DEUTERONOMY 30:1–10; 18:15–19

Think Through the Questions:

1. Why do you think these passages are so important?
2. What does it mean to be a "priestly kingdom? What does it mean to be a "holy nation"?
3. In what way do these passages develop the metanarrative (the big Story) begun in Genesis 12:1–3?
4. What new elements are added to this Story by these passages?

Summarize the Core Teaching of the Passages:

Write a paragraph, outline, annotate, or chart your conclusions—whatever best communicates for you.

Core teaching of Exodus 19:1–6; 20:1–17; Deuteronomy 30:1–10; 18:15–19:

Consult the Scholars

The following comments are designed to help you better understand the passages and to stimulate your thinking on the implications of the teaching.

Read and Reflect on this Brief Commentary on Exodus 19:1–6; 20:1–17; Deuteronomy 30:1–10; 18:15–19

As we saw in the last session, God promised to make a great nation out of Abraham and his descendants. In these passages we see the formation of that nation. Also, as we saw in Peter's sermon last week (Acts 3:11–26), Peter moved from Abraham in Genesis 12:1–3 to Moses, who spoke of a coming prophet to whom everyone needed to listen. If they did not, they would be cut off from the nation God had formed to bless all the families of the earth. Who was this Moses? How does he fit into the Story? Well remember, God promised to make a great nation out of Abraham, and Moses played the key role in the formation of that nation.

Narration: What happened between the promises of Genesis 12:1–3 and the formation of the promised nation?
- The Story unfolds (from Abraham to Moses).
- Abraham has 2 sons: Ishmael and Isaac.
- Isaac has 2 sons: Jacob and Esau.
- Jacob has 12 sons, who became the nation of Israel.
- Israel is put into slavery by Egypt for 400 years.
- God raises up Moses, who leads then out of Egypt, across the Red Sea to Mount Sinai, where he makes a covenant with Israel.
- It is here, at Mount Sinai, that God gives them the Law, in essence the constitution of the nation, embedded in the Abrahamic promise to bless all the families of the earth. Genesis 19:1–6 is actually the formalization of the formation of the nation in covenant form.

Now God develops the promise further at Mount Sinai, when He calls Abraham up to the mountain and gives him the Law. Exodus 19:1–6 is a clear statement of continuity of the promise—God develops it further (the house of Jacob shows the continuous development).

> 19:1 On the third new moon after the Israelites had gone out of the land of Egypt, on that very day, they came into the wilderness of Sinai. ² They had journeyed from Rephidim, entered the wilderness of Sinai, and camped in the wilderness; Israel camped there in front of the mountain. ³ Then Moses went up to God; the Lord called to him from the mountain, saying, "Thus you shall say to the house of Jacob, and tell the Israelites: ⁴ You have seen what I did to the Egyptians, and how I bore you on eagles' wings and brought you to myself. ⁵ Now therefore, if you obey my voice and keep my covenant, you shall be my treasured possession out of all the peoples. Indeed, the whole earth is mine, ⁶ but you shall be for me a priestly kingdom and a holy nation. These are the words that you shall speak to the Israelites."

Let's make several observations in God's communication to Moses. The key idea: Israel is to be a "priestly kingdom and a holy nation," if they keep His covenant. They will be a priestly kingdom (among the nations)—a nation between God and the nations—introducing God to the nations…if they keep His covenant. So the Law, the Mosaic Covenant, is embedded in the promise given to Abraham and is intended to guide them into becoming the kind of nation that can represent God to the nations. Therefore, they must be a holy nation, guided by His principles and laws. In Exodus 20:1–17, He gives them His core principles—the Ten Commandments.

The Ten Commandments (the first principles of the Law)
1. You shall not worship any other gods but YHWH (the Hebrew name for God).
2. You shall not make for yourself an idol.
3. You shall not make wrongful use of the Lord's name (YHWH).

4. Remember the Sabbath day and keep it holy (rest every 7th day).
5. Honor your father and mother.
6. Do not murder.
7. Do not commit adultery.
8. Do not steal.
9. Do not falsely accuse your neighbor.
10. Do not covet your neighbor—his wife or his possessions.

Key idea: These ten commandments are the foundational principles of the covenant. They are in essence *the first principles* of the covenant. If the nation obeyed them, they would be "a priestly kingdom and a holy nation." This is a significant part of God's grand strategy for the history of mankind. The concept of a *grand strategy* has a deep history in global literature. I have books on the grand strategy of the Roman Empire and the grand strategy of the Byzantine Empire. I have major research on the grand strategy for the resurgence of the USA since WWI, which I am not recommending, but it is big-time research. One of the observations in grand strategy research is that the strategy must be based on a set of founding or *first principles* (see Kaiser's quote).

But for now, let's continue with the narrative of God's Story.

Narration continues: The Story from Exodus to Deuteronomy:

- In the rest of Exodus and Leviticus, the details of the Mosaic covenant—the Law—are recorded in detail.
- In Numbers, the nation of Israel wanders in the wilderness for 40 years after their disobedience.
- In Deuteronomy, the Mosaic covenant is given a second time, finishing with chapters 28–30, in which a future of blessings and curses is predicted, based on their obedience and disobedience.

The key passage is Deuteronomy 30:1–10. The key idea: The nation will have periods of obeying and disobeying the Law, but in the future God will change their hearts, which is the only way they will ever fulfill the covenant God made with them through Moses. Deuteronomy 18:15–19 is also a very important passage. A prophet will come in the future, in the tradition of Moses, through whom God will explain everything and to whom the nation should listen.

Now let's go back to Peter's sermon—Acts 3:17–21. Peter understands that Jesus fulfilled the prophecy of a prophet being raised up, in the tradition of Moses, through whom God would explain everything . . . and by implication, bring in fully the promise of a coming kingdom.

Now we are ready to summarize the additional elements of the unfolding Story—God's plan—His grand strategy for the history of mankind.

God's Plan for the History of Mankind

1. God made a covenant with Israel, the nation promised to Abraham, to bless all the families of the earth through them.
2. His intention was for that nation to be a nation that introduced God to the nations—"a priestly kingdom and a holy nation."
3. At the foundation of the nation was a set of first principles (the Ten Commandments), designed to guide them as a nation, set apart for God.
4. They would not be able to obey the covenant until a future time when God would change their hearts permanently.
5. In the future, a prophet would come, in the tradition of Moses, through whom God would explain everything. Peter saw this prophet as Jesus.

See Appendix A for an accumulated summary of the Story (God's grand strategy as it is unfolding session by session.) At the end of each session and before the new session begins, review the appendix.

Read and Reflect on Key Quotes:

This continues the quote by Walter Kaiser from his work *Recovering the Unity of the Bible: One Continuous Story, Plan, and Purpose*. In this quote, Kaiser shares his conclusions on the validity of a continuous story, plan, and purpose as he looks at some of the main historic epochs of biblical history. This session looks at the time of the exodus.

"**The time of the exodus.** After the four hundred years between the time of the patriarchs and the events of the exodus, the promise of the covenant was freshly restated once again. It expressly perpetuated the offers given to Abraham (Ex. 2:24: 'God heard their groaning and he remembered his covenant with Abraham, with Isaac and with Jacob'; also Ex. 3:13, 15–16; 6:3–5; Deut. 4:31). It was at this time that God took the Israelites 'as [his] own people' (Ex. 6:7; 29:45; Lev. 11:45; 22:33; 25:38; 26:12, 45; Num. 15:41; Deut. 26:17–19; 29:12–13). In fact, God's intention was to make them all into a 'kingdom of priests and a holy nation' (Ex. 19:5–6). Disappointingly, Israel shrunk back from this call to be a priesthood of believers and begged Moses instead to go into the presence of God to get God's Word, for the experience of having God speak to them from heaven was altogether too awesome and frightening—fire, lightning, thunder, and all! Thus, this mediatorial task of the whole body of the people was delayed until New Testament times (1 Peter 2:5, 9; Rev. 1:6; 5:10).

"Nevertheless, Israel was to be Yahweh's 'Son.' This special relationship was not mentioned very often, but it was part of the same promise-plan (Ex. 4:22–23; Deut. 1:31; 32:6). Here again, the eternal and irrevocable aspects of the promise were stressed (Ex. 3:15; Deut. 4:40; 12:28). To be sure, *personal* participation in the promise covenant was conditioned on obedience (e.g., Deut. 4:40; 12:28), yet the promise itself was depicted as being irrevocable. In Leviticus 26:44–45 the Lord says: 'Yet in spite of this, when they are in the land of their enemies, I will not reject them or abhor them so as to destroy them completely, breaking my covenant with them. I am the LORD their God. But for their sake I will remember the covenant with their ancestors whom I brought out of Egypt' (NASB; see also Deut. 4:30–31)."[7]

Record any insights from the brief commentary and quotes:

Think Through the Issues

As the Story unfolds, historically, it needs to be true. The nation of Israel is the nation promised by God to Abraham in Genesis 12:1–3. Peter quotes from the Genesis passage. He also quotes from Deuteronomy 18 when referring to Jesus as the prophet Moses talked about. One of the most basic questions we must ask is, "Is the Bible historically true?" In this section, we will reflect on the historical reliability of the Story. There must be a nation of Israel. The purpose of the nation, and its passions, must match the reason for its creation. It must match its ups and downs—it's blessings and curses. History must match its attempts at obeying the covenants, its renewal by men and women attempting to fulfill its covenants. It must record its failings and the curses from those failures must be recorded. In this section we will think through its reliability.

ISSUE: The historical reliability of the Story

Think Through the Issue Before Discussion:

1. As the Story unfolds, do you find it credible?
2. In what way is the historical nature of the kerygma—the gospel story—an apologetic in and of itself?
3. Is Peter using the Deuteronomy quote correctly? How does his use of the passage, weaving it with Genesis 12:1–3, build credibility?

Record your initial thoughts on the issue before discussion:

Discuss the issue in your small group.

Record your initial thoughts on the issue after discussion:

Apply the Principles

It is now time to respond to what you have studied and discussed. Take your time on this section.

Think Back Through the First Three Steps.

Design an Application for Your Life.

The Story needs to be credible. The nation of Israel is in the news worldwide today and has been central to world history through the centuries. In order for the Story to be credible it must be true to real history. Record your thoughts on how the story of the nation of Israel throughout history adds to the historical credibility of the Story.

THE DAVIDIC COVENANT ❺

Remember, the way we are recreating the Story Jesus told on the road to Damascus is by listening to how the Apostles told the Story (which they understood because Jesus opened their minds to understand the Scriptures). We now turn our attention to David, the next major figure in the Story as interpreted by Jesus. We know this because Paul included David in the Story he shared at the synagogue, as recorded in Acts 13:13–41, which we looked at briefly in session one.

Paul describes the covenant God made with David by giving his own summary of Israel's history up to David and then focusing on the significance of David and God's covenant with him. Paul refers to God as finding David, a man after His own heart. In this section, we will examine the narrative in 2 Samuel, where God makes a covenant with David. Then we will look at several of the Psalms David wrote that point to the coming of Jesus. We will again ask whether the Apostles' use of the Scriptures (Paul in this case) is accurate. It will lead us to a fuller understanding of the unfolding promise and grand strategy and to further opening our minds to understanding the Scriptures.

Study the Scriptures
READ THE PASSAGES: 2 SAMUEL 7:1–29; ISAIAH 9:1–7; PSALM 89:1–4, 30–37; PSALM 16:8–11; PSALM 110:1–6; AND ISAIAH 9:1–7

Think Through the Questions:

1. Why do you think these passages are so important?
2. What does it mean that both David's house and kingdom will be established forever?
3. In what way do these passages help develop the metanarrative established in Genesis 12:1–3?
4. What new elements are added to the Story by these passages?

Summarize the Core Teaching of the Passages:

Write a paragraph, outline, annotate, or chart your conclusions—whatever best communicates for you.

Core teaching of 2 Samuel 7:1–29; Isaiah 9:1–7; Psalm 89:1–4, 30–37; Psalm 16:8–11; Psalm 110:1–6; and Isaiah 9:1–7:

Consult the Scholars

The following comments are designed to help you better understand the passages and to stimulate your thinking on the implications of the teaching.

Read and Reflect on this Brief Commentary on 2 Samuel 7:1–29; Isaiah 9:1–7; Psalm 89:1–4, 30–37; Psalm 16:8–11; Psalm 110:1–6; and Isaiah 9:1–7

First, review Appendix A—the Story so far.

In the last session, we saw how God fulfilled His promise to make a great nation from Abraham and his descendants by working through Moses and making a covenant with Israel. In the passages in this session, we will see how God continued to develop and carry out His promise made to Abraham and his descendants by promising a king from the line of David, who would make it possible for God to bless all the nations through Abraham's descendants.

We now turn our attention to the main narrative, 2 Samuel 7:1–29, where God develops His promise, first made to Abraham in Genesis 12:1–3, by focusing on the promised seed that will come through his descendants. But first let's review the narrative from Moses to David.

Storyline after the second giving of the Law in Deuteronomy:
- God raised up Joshua to lead them back into the land.
- God raised up judges to rule to keep Israel on the right course, through ups and downs.
- They demanded a king, so God relented.
- Saul was the first king (evil).
- David was the second king.

The interchange between God and David, through the prophet Nathan, is very interesting, almost humorous. Once David is successful as Israel's king, he decides he is going to do something for God. He wants to build Him a temple, since God has been dwelling in a big tent since He gave the Law to Moses. But God humbles David by first telling him that He never commanded David to build a house for Him. He reminds David that He made him who he is (he was a shepherd before God got a hold of him), and furthermore, it is David's son Solomon who will build the temple for God. God then reverses the image by saying that He is going to build David a house—his house (family line), his kingdom, and his throne will last forever.

The key contribution to the Story:

God made 3 promises to David:
- His house (lineage) would last forever.
- His kingdom would be established forever.
- The king over this kingdom would be an extension of his throne—a king from the line of David would reign over this everlasting kingdom.

The Story then continues in 7:18 and following. David was humbled by the interchange with God through the prophet Nathan. David then goes before God and confesses his arrogance. In that confession, he reflects upon the significance of what God just promised him. God states that it is because of His promise to Abraham that He is making this covenant with David and his house. David fully realizes that God is a great God, showing everyone His love for mankind through Abraham; through Israel, the great nation He created; and through this promise to him. He then prays for God to carry out this promise.

The key contribution to the Story:

What did David understand about these promises?
- He understood this was very significant, and it needed to be included in the Scriptures—"instruction to the people."
- He understood God is making a great name for Himself through His people Israel.

- David prays it will be accomplished, and he ties it to God making a "great nation."

Isaiah 9:1–7 is another key passage that builds on the covenant with David. It is an outstanding example of what Jesus was doing when He opened the minds of the disciples on the road to Emmaus, and it gives a proof of the Scriptures all pointing to Him. We do not have time to review much about the book of Isaiah here. Isaiah was one of the great prophets in *the Prophets*, the second section of the Scriptures. In the beginning of the book, Isaiah deals with the nations for rejecting God and His plan. He then deals with Israel's failure to live up to the covenant God made with them at Sinai, but then in chapters 40–66 Isaiah focuses on the promise God made to bless all the families of the earth and how He would bring it about. Embedded in this last section are "The Songs of the Servant," four sections, written in poetic form (42:1–4; etc.). In these songs, Isaiah gives a detailed picture of the coming Messiah, including the death of this Messiah on the cross. It is amazing prophetic detail. Let's look briefly at Isaiah 9:1–7, a detailed prophesy of this coming Davidic king.

The key contribution of this prophecy to the Story:

This king
- will be born from David's line.
- will come from Galilee.
- will be both God and man ("mighty God," "eternal father").
- will rule over David's throne and kingdom forever.

The Psalms—there are 150 of them all together. They are located at the beginning of the third section of the Jewish Scriptures (in our Bible it's the "Old Testament") called *the Writings*. They are so significant that sometimes this third section of the Scriptures is referred to as the Psalms—the Law, the Prophets, and the Psalms.

The Psalms make key contributions to the Story:

- David knew this promise—covenant—God made to him needed to be built into the Story.
- David built several Psalms around this instruction; Psalms 16 and 110 are key examples of this.
- Psalm 89, written by Ethan the Ezrahite, continued this tradition.

Psalm 89 is a very long Psalm, which unfolds the theology of the 2 Samuel 7 passage.

> [1] I will sing of your steadfast love, O Lord, forever;
> with my mouth I will proclaim your faithfulness to all generations.
> [2] I declare that your steadfast love is established forever;
> your faithfulness is as firm as the heavens.
> [3] You said, "I have made a covenant with my chosen one,
> I have sworn to my servant David:
> [4] 'I will establish your descendants forever,

and build your throne for all generations.' " Psalm 89:1–4

³⁰ If his children forsake my law
  and do not walk according to my ordinances,
³¹ if they violate my statutes
  and do not keep my commandments,
³² then I will punish their transgression with the rod
  and their iniquity with scourges;
³³ but I will not remove from him my steadfast love,
  or be false to my faithfulness.
³⁴ I will not violate my covenant,
  or alter the word that went forth from my lips.
³⁵ Once and for all I have sworn by my holiness;
  I will not lie to David.
³⁶ His line shall continue forever,
  and his throne endure before me like the sun.
³⁷ It shall be established forever like the moon,
  an enduring witness in the skies."

Psalm 89:30–37

What additional does Psalm 89:1–4 add to the Story?

Building on Deuteronomy 30:1–10
- God will discipline Israel in the future as they disobey.
- But because of His promise (lovingkindness), God will establish David's kingdom and throne (Israel) forever (v. 4 "build up.")

What does Psalm 89:30–37 add to the Story?
- Ethan called these promises a covenant with David.
- His seed—lineage—will last forever.
- The king of this coming kingdom will come from David's seed.
- Because of God's lovingkindness, this throne and kingdom "will be built up" (vv. 36–37) by God over many generations for all generations.

Now let's refer back to Paul's speech in Acts 13:13–41 and look at Peter's speech in Acts 2. Paul refers to the Psalms and so does Peter, backing up Dodd's theory that the Apostles all used the same storyline and several key passages again and again to validate the Story as Jesus told it on the road to Emmaus. Paul refers to Isaiah 55 (one of Isaiah's "Songs of the Servant") and Psalms 2 and 16; Peter refers to Psalms 16 and 110. Both of them refer to Psalms 16. In Peter's first sermon, why does he quote from Psalms 16 and 110? He is proving from the Old Testament that Jesus is the one spoken of by David. In those two Psalms—16 and 110—David is building off the covenant God made with him. Let's look at excerpts from both Psalms.

⁸ I keep the Lord always before me;
  because he is at my right hand, I shall not be moved.

⁹ Therefore my heart is glad, and my soul rejoices;
   my body also rests secure.
¹⁰ For you do not give me up to Sheol,
   or let your faithful one to undergo decay.
¹¹ You show me the path of life.
   In your presence there is fullness of joy;
   in your right hand are pleasures forevermore.

Psalms 16:8–11

What did David understand?

- God would not abandon him or His promise.
- The holy one (his Lord) would not undergo decay, thus foreseeing the resurrection according to Peter.

And Psalms 110

¹ The Lord says to my lord,
  "Sit at my right hand
  until I make your enemies your footstool."
² The Lord sends out from Zion
  your mighty scepter.
  Rule in the midst of your foes.
³ Your people will offer themselves willingly
  on the day you lead your forces
  on the holy mountains.
  From the womb of the morning,
  like dew, your youth will come to you.
⁴ The Lord has sworn and will not change his mind,
  "You are a priest forever according to the order of Melchizedek."
⁵ The Lord is at your right hand;
  he will shatter kings on the day of his wrath.
⁶ He will execute judgment among the nations,
  filling them with corpses;

Psalm 110:1–6

What did David understand?

- David understood that the future king from his seed would sit at the right hand of God.
- David referred to him as his Lord.

Did David really understand all of this? (See Kaiser in the Quotes section of this session.)

Now we can add to the unfolding Story of the plan of God—His grand strategy.

The Plan for the History of Mankind (developed further)

- God made a covenant with David that his kingdom and his throne would last forever.

- The future king would come from Galilee and would be both God and man.
- David foresaw this king as his Lord and that He would not undergo decay but would sit at the right hand of God (predicting the resurrection).
- David saw this as part of the plan of God, of making Israel a great nation and of making a great name for Himself, and David used the Psalms to build this instruction into the people of God.

Read and Reflect on Key Quotes:

The following quote continues the selection from Walter Kaiser that we began in session 3, from his work *Recovering the Unity of the Bible: One Continuous Story, Plan and Purpose*. This time we are covering the period of David and the post-Davidic times.

"***The time of David.*** In preparation for the throne of David to be set up, God began to give 'rest' from all of Israel's enemies as he chose a 'place' for his 'name to dwell' among the people (Deut. 12:9–10, 14, 21; 25:19). This elusive 'rest' was partially fulfilled at the time of the division of the land, as recorded in Deuteronomy 3:20, and in the work of the leader Joshua (Josh. 1:13). It is mentioned again in Psalm 95:11. This divine work of God was another link that connected the time of the exodus with that of David.

"The classic passage that supplied the next advance in the promise-plan of God came in 2 Samuel 7, with its account of David's proposal to the prophet Nathan for building a temple for Yahweh. But instead of David building a 'house' for Yahweh, God would make a 'house,' that is, a 'dynasty,' out of David (vv. 5, 10–11). The details in the promise seemed to be as numerous as they were in the promise given to Abraham. They included the following: (1) God would establish a 'house' that consisted of a line of descendants that would come forth from David and sit on his throne (vv. 12, 16, 19, 25, 26, 29). (2) One of those descendants would build the temple for Yahweh that David had proposed. (3) The seed of David would reign in God's kingdom as a whole line of rulers who would succeed him (vv. 12, 13, 16). (4) This reign would extend into all eternity (vv. 13, 16, 25, 26, 29). (5) This promise to David was again declared to be irrevocable even if he sinned (vv. 14–15; cf. 1 Chron. 28:7; Ps. 132:12). (6) Finally, this promise was to be what I call a 'charter for all humanity' (Heb., torat ha'adam) (v. 19), concluding exactly where the Abraham covenant climaxed with its 'in your seed all the nations of the earth shall be blessed'—the missions aspect of the promise! This expression is often given strange translations in English texts, but what God was going to do would be a 'law' or a 'charter' for everyone in the world to enjoy by faith, if they would. It, too, would act just as the climactic note in the Abrahamic covenant was aimed—a provision for all the nations.

"***The post-Davidic times.*** Up to this point, the view garnered from the earliest times to the times of David is that Yahweh has made Israel his distinctive people, and he has vested this relationship centrally in the royal line of David. Yahweh's purpose for doing this, however, was to bring blessing to all humanity. Added to this picture is the preaching of the prophets, who declared that this one promise was being fulfilled in their times; yet it also remained to be fulfilled largely in the future, in the person of the Messiah—a 'now' and a 'not yet' inaugurated eschatology.

"The prophets spoke of Israel as the people of promise. While they could treat Israel merely as a nation or as a race of mortals, they could also distinguish a true Israel within Israel who had, like Abraham, believed in that coming Man of Promise. Moreover, all nations had an interest in the promise, for there was no other deliverance coming from any other source except through the promise God had given in this line established in Israel. This extension of the good news to all the nations could be seen in Solomon's prayer at the dedication of the temple (1 Kings 8:41–43; 2 Chron. 6:32–33), and in numerous formal repetitions in the Psalms and the Prophets (Ps. 72:17; Isa. 49:6–7; 65:16; Jer. 4:1–2; Zech. 14:16). But amazingly the promise was continuously declared to be eternal and irrevocable (1 Kings 11:36; 2 Chron. 21:7; Ps. 89:26–37; Isa. 59:20–21).

"During the prophetic eras, certain words came to take on a partly technical usage in the teaching of the promise doctrine. The roots of several of these terms was often pre-Davidic, with strong development of them in the Psalms. The one surprising term, however, was *messiah*. This term appears some thirty-nine times in the older testament, yet in no more than nine of the thirty-nine instances does it possibly refer to the Messiah (1 Sam. 2:10, 35; Ps. 2:2; 20:6; 28:8; 84:9; Dan. 9:25, 26; Hab. 3:13). On the other hand, by all odds, the most prominent technical term for the special descendant of David was 'the Servant of the Lord.' It had been used in a nontechnical way of Moses, Caleb, Samson, and Nebuchadnezzar throughout Scripture, but it is with David that the term *servant* begins to take on a technical status. The term also is used of Israel (Isa. 41:8, 9; 44:1, 2, 21; 45:4; 48:20; 49:3). When the term *servant* is applied technically to Israel or to the line of David, it speaks of them either as the promise people or as the promise dynasty (Isa. 49:5–7; Rom. 9:6–8). Therefore we say that the servant is Israel, yet the servant is also Jesus, who is the highest disclosure of Yahweh himself, in and through the people of Israel. Other technical terms can be added to 'anointed one/Messiah' and 'servant.' We have already mentioned Seed,' 'Son,' and 'firstborn.' Add to these the 'Chosen One,' the 'Holy One (Heb., hasid), the 'Branch' (Heb., tsemah), 'Shoot' (Heb., netser), the 'lamp,' and the 'star' and the picture of Messiah in the Old Testament begins to broaden extensively."[8]

Record any insights from the brief commentary and quotes:

 ## Think Through the Issues

Again, it is critical as this Story unfolds that it rings true historically. In his first sermon, Peter quotes from two Psalms—16 and 110—to validate to the nation of Israel, that all that is unfolding was predicted and validated by the "Old Testament" Scriptures. It is the heart of his extensive sermon at Pentecost, demonstrating from the Scriptures that Jesus is the promised Messiah and King in the Davidic promises. He claims that David understood that this coming King from his lineage was the Lord himself. Was Peter accurate? Did he use the Old Testament correctly? If he did, then this is tremendous validation of the whole of the Scriptures pointing to Jesus as the coming King who would inaugurate the coming kingdom promised to David. This is an enormous validation of the historical Jesus. It gives us a map for understanding the nations and their eventual incorporation into Christ's kingdom. We will explore the implications of all of these realities in this session.

ISSUE: Validation of the gospel story (kerygma) in the covenant with David

Think Through the Issue Before Discussion:

1. As the Story unfolds, do you find it credible?
2. In what way is the historical nature of the kerygma—the gospel story—an apologetic in and of itself?
3. Is Peter using Psalms correctly? How does all of this validate the events around Christ's death and resurrection?
4. In what sense, then, is the kerygma validated as the inauguration of the coming kingdom?
5. How critical is it to be on a lifetime journey toward mastering the Scriptures?

> Record your initial thoughts on the issue before discussion:

Discuss the issue in your small group.

Record your initial thoughts on the issue after discussion:

Apply the Principles

It is now time to respond to what you have studied and discussed. Take your time on this section.

Think Back Through the First Three Steps.

Design an Application for Your Life.

Think through the covenant of David and the incredible predictions of the coming of a Davidic king. Record your thoughts on whether these passages accurately predict the coming of the Davidic king and how Jesus fulfilled these promises. Are these passages proofs of the credibility of the Story? Also record the effect of these realities on strengthening your own faith.

THE KINGDOM ARRIVES 6

In the last session, we saw that a king would come from David's line who would establish the kingdom of God forever. He would be both God and man. He would come as a light to the Gentiles and would come from a more remote area, from Galilee, beyond the Jordan. We saw that this king would set up God's kingdom, thus fulfilling His promise to bless all the families of the earth through Abraham and his descendants. This promise was fully developed in the promise to David and his lineage.

As we examine these passages in the book of Mark, we will look for whether the Scriptures really do point to Jesus and whether Jesus fulfills the prophecies in the Jewish Scriptures. We will ask the questions of whether Jesus' self understanding of who He was, is accurate. This will go a long way to answering the question of whether His understanding is accurate with the prophecies of the Old Testament and then answering the questions facing each of us: whether to believe in Jesus as our Savior, whether to believe the Story is true, and whether we too should become followers of this Jesus—this bright light to the Gentiles who calls people into His kingdom.

Study the Scriptures
READ THE PASSAGES: KEY TEXT: MARK 1:1–15
COROLLARY TEXTS: MARK 8:27–31; 9:30–32; 10:32–34; 12:35–37; 14:22–25; 16:14–18; ACTS 10:34–43; 1 CORINTHIANS 15:1–6; OLD TESTAMENT VALIDATION TEXTS: ISAIAH 53:1–12 (SONGS OF THE SERVANT)

Think Through the Questions:

1. Why do you think Mark 1:1–15 is so important?
2. What does it mean that the kingdom of God is at hand?
3. In what way does this passage help develop the metanarrative established in Genesis 12:1–3?
4. What new elements are added to the Story by this passage?

Grasping the Metanarrative in a Postmodern World

Summarize the Core Teaching of the Passages:

Summarize what Mark 1:1–15 adds to the promise, and comment on why the statement that the kingdom of God is near is so important to understanding the storyline of the Scriptures—the Law, the Prophets, and the Writings. Try to identify the role of this passage in the overall plan, which will eventually include all the nations of the earth.

> Core teaching of key texts: Mark 1:1–15; 8:27–31; 9:30–32; 10:32–34; 12:35–37; 14:22–25; 16:14–18; Isaiah 53:1–12; Acts 10:34–43; 1 Corinthians 15:1–6:

 # Consult the Scholars

The following comments are designed to help you better understand the passage and to stimulate your thinking on the implications of the teaching.

Read and Reflect on this Brief Commentary on Mark 1:1–15; 8:27–31; 9:30–32; 10:32–34; 12:35–37; 14:22–25; 16:14–18; Isaiah 53:1–12; Acts 10:34–43; 1 Corinthians 15:1–6:

First, review Appendix A—the Story so far.

As we saw in the last session, a king would come from David's line who would sit on the throne of God's coming kingdom. This king would reign forever over God's kingdom and, in that sense, would cause David's throne to last forever. The coming of that king is described in the four Gospels: Matthew, Mark, Luke, and John. We chose the Gospel of

Mark to examine the coming of that king. We will begin with the first fifteen verses of Mark. Mark chose to begin with a quote from Isaiah 40, again following the pattern of the Apostles and their team validating Jesus by showing how the Scriptures pointed to Jesus as the promised king. John the Baptist was that prophet announcing that the coming was now. Three phrases are used in Mark 1:1 and 1:14–15 that are critical to understanding the announcement.

Three key "Story" phrases:

"the good news of Jesus Christ"
good news—"euangelion"—modern day term for evangelism; it is the good news concerning Jesus Christ

"proclaiming the good news of Jesus Christ"
proclaiming—a form of "kerygma"—term used for preaching, announcing, making known—ancient term for *the kerygma*—the content of the good news

"the kingdom of God has come near"
near—is approaching; "Time is fulfilled" = come to an end

Think back to the road to Emmaus. Jesus and the kingdom are tied together right at the beginning of Mark's account of the gospel. John the Baptist makes it clear that he is announcing the king of the Davidic promises, thus the promised descendant from Abraham's descendants who would bless all the families of the earth.

This passage adds significantly to the Story—the further unfolding of God's plan.
1. The kingdom of God, as promised in the Old Testament, is now near at hand.
2. The good news of this coming kingdom is being proclaimed, and it is about Jesus Christ.
3. Jesus Christ is identified as the Son of God (remember Isaiah), and God himself identifies Him as His Son.
4. He is the light from Galilee (remember Isaiah)—the coming king from David's line will be both God and man.

As Mark unfolds, Jesus predicts His coming death, burial, and resurrection four times. The first three are almost in formula form; the last one is just before His crucifixion.

> "²⁷ Jesus went on with his disciples to the villages of Caesarea Philippi; and on the way he asked his disciples, "Who do people say that I am?" ²⁸ And they answered him, "John the Baptist; and others, Elijah; and still others, one of the prophets." ²⁹ He asked them, "But who do you say that I am?" Peter answered him, "You are the Messiah." ³⁰ And he sternly ordered them not to tell anyone about him. ³¹ Then he began to teach them that the Son of Man must undergo great suffering, and be rejected by the elders, the chief priests, and the scribes, and be killed, and after three days rise again." Mark 8:27–31

³⁰ They went on from there and passed through Galilee. He did not want anyone to know it; ³¹ for he was teaching his disciples, saying to them, "The Son of Man is to be betrayed into human hands, and they will kill him, and three days after being killed, he will rise again." ³² But they did not understand what he was saying and were afraid to ask him. Mark 9:30–32

³² They were on the road, going up to Jerusalem, and Jesus was walking ahead of them; they were amazed, and those who followed were afraid. He took the twelve aside again and began to tell them what was to happen to him, ³³ saying, "See, we are going up to Jerusalem, and the Son of Man will be handed over to the chief priests and the scribes, and they will condemn him to death; then they will hand him over to the Gentiles; ³⁴ they will mock him, and spit upon him, and flog him, and kill him; and after three days he will rise again." Mark 10:32–34

These three predictions form a kind of formula.

Prediction formula in Mark: Jesus must suffer, be rejected, be killed, and rise again the third day. This forms the heart of the proclamation of the good news called the *kerygma*.

Now we go to the end of Mark, where we see Jesus eating the Last Supper with the disciples before His crucifixion, when this prediction will be fulfilled. In John's Gospel, Jesus uses the term a *New Covenant* He is making with them. This is followed by His final prediction of His death, burial, and resurrection.

²² While they were eating, he took a loaf of bread, and after blessing it he broke it, gave it to them, and said, "Take; this is my body." ²³ Then he took a cup, and after giving thanks he gave it to them, and all of them drank from it. ²⁴ He said to them, "This is my blood of the covenant, which is poured out for many. ²⁵ Truly I tell you, I will never again drink of the fruit of the vine until that day when I drink it new in the kingdom of God." Mark 14:22–25

At the Last Supper, before the predicted event of His death, burial, and resurrection, Jesus took the cup and tied it to a New Covenant He was making with them. He states He will not drink of it again until He drinks it with them in the coming kingdom. This New Covenant was prophesied by Jeremiah.

³¹ The days are surely coming, says the Lord, when I will make a new covenant with the house of Israel and the house of Judah. ³² It will not be like the covenant that I made with their ancestors when I took them by the hand to bring them out of the land of Egypt—a covenant that they broke, though I was their husband, says the Lord. ³³ But this is the covenant that I will make with the house of Israel after those days, says the Lord: I will put my law within them, and I will write it on their hearts; and I will be their God, and they shall be my people. ³⁴ No longer shall they teach one another, or say to each other, "Know the Lord," for they shall all know me,

> from the least of them to the greatest, says the Lord; for I will forgive their iniquity, and remember their sin no more." Jeremiah 31:31–34

The essence of Jeremiah's prophecy is this:
1. It is a New Covenant the Lord will make with Israel.
2. He will change their hearts.
3. He will forgive their sins.

Now we turn to our last passage in Mark, where Jesus makes clear the full content of the announcement by John the Baptist, and then by Himself, which we saw in Mark 1:1 and 1:14–15.

> [14] Later he appeared to the eleven themselves as they were sitting at the table; and he upbraided them for their lack of faith and stubbornness, because they had not believed those who saw him after he had risen. [15] And he said to them, "Go into all the world and proclaim the good news to the whole creation. [16] The one who believes and is baptized will be saved; but the one who does not believe will be condemned. Mark 16:14–16

This passage ties together the proclamation of the good news of Jesus—His death, burial, and resurrection—with the kingdom being at hand. He inaugurates the kingdom by sending His disciples to all the world. Jesus' death, burial, and resurrection are tied to the beginning of this kingdom and the beginning of the specific mission to bless all the families of the earth. Many today call it *The Great Commission*.

Before we focus on this good news announced by John and Jesus, let's go back again to the four "Songs of the Servant" we talked about earlier in Isaiah. They give a detailed picture of this suffering the coming King must go through before the kingdom can be inaugurated, leading to all the families of the earth being blessed. Isaiah 53 is the greatest of these prophecies. This "song of the Servant" prophesies that the promised coming king must suffer and die for the sins of the world. The essence of the song is this:

This servant
1. will be filled with suffering.
2. will die for the sins of others.
3. will be made great in the future, by God.

What is this good news John and Jesus announced? Now we are ready to make that clear. Jesus summarized it in His commission to go and proclaim the good news to the world. Peter was the first to proclaim it. This good news—the gospel proclaimed by Jesus and what the Early Church called *the kerygma*—was summarized by Peter in his 5 sermons (proclamations) in Acts. Peter's simplest summary is in Acts 10:34–43, at Cornelius' home. This is the essence of his proclamations:
- Jesus Christ was the promised king of the Old Testament prophecies, who would bring in the kingdom God promised to Israel.

- He must be rejected, killed, buried, and resurrected to cover the sins of those who would be part of this kingdom.
- Those who believe and have their sins forgiven are part of this new kingdom and are sent out to proclaim this message to the whole world.

And that is what the disciples went out and did: They proclaimed the good news—the gospel of Jesus Christ.

Peter and Paul both summarized the proclamation of this good news. Paul describes this proclamation as a tradition handed down to him from the Apostles, in a formula-like statement, which he calls *the gospel*. Paul's summary is in 1 Corinthians 15:1–6. It is the good news that the Corinthians believed and then they were saved. The essence is this:
- Christ died for our sins according to the Scriptures.
- He was buried and raised on the third day according to the Scriptures.
- He appeared to Peter and then to the 12 and then to more than 500.

In fact, through the Gospel of Mark, Peter shapes the ministry of Jesus and His time on earth as almost entirely kerygmatic. So again, what was the essence of this good news called the *kerygma* or the *gospel*?

Jesus Christ, the promised king and son of God, came down and lived life on earth as a man; went about doing good and healing; was rejected by Israel; was killed, buried, and resurrected; and before He ascended, commissioned His followers to take this message to the entire world; then ascended to heaven to sit at the right hand of God, until He returns, sets up the kingdom, and enjoys the supper once again, but then with all of His followers.

Now let's put the whole picture together.

The Plan for the History of Mankind (developed further)

1. Jesus arrived on the scene, proclaiming the good news (the kerygma): the kingdom of God is at hand.
2. Jesus identified Himself as the Son of God, the coming king promised in the prophecies of the Old Testament.
3. The essence of that good news was revealed: He would be killed, buried, and resurrected, and those who believe in Him would be part of His kingdom.
4. Those who believed, a small group of followers who remained with Him after His resurrection and ascension, were to proclaim this good news, this gospel, to the whole world. (Remember Genesis 12:1–3.)
5. Peter proclaimed this gospel in early Acts in 5 sermons.
6. Paul stated this gospel—the good news—in formula form and affirmed having received it from the Apostles.

Read and Reflect on Key Quotes:

In this session, we continue the quote that began in Session 3 which traces the main historic epochs of biblical history from the Old Testament to the New Testament. It's the quote from Walter Kaiser from his work *Recovering the Unity of the Bible: One Continuous Story, Plan, and Purpose*. This session concludes our chosen quote with "the times of fulfillment" and "the time of the arrival of the promise."

"***The times of fulfillment.*** No less certain were the New Testament writers that the single, definite promise from God was the theme not only of the older testament, but of the times of fulfillment as well. When Stephen stood before the Sanhedrin, he, too, traced that same path: 'Brothers and fathers, listen to me! The God of glory appeared to our father Abraham while he was still in Mesopotamia, before he lived in Haran. "Leave your country and your people," God said, "and go to the land I will show you."… As the time drew near for God to fulfill his promise to Abraham, the number of our people in Egypt greatly increased' (Acts 7:2–3, 17).

"Despite the fact that the Old Testament does not use the term *promise*, it does possess the concept in a constellation of Hebrew terms, such as *blessing*, *oath*, *pledge*, and the like. Moreover, the writers of the New Testament adopted the Old Testament phraseology as their own way of expressing God's revelation to them. Routinely they appealed to concepts, such as 'the last days,' 'the day of the Lord,' 'the Servant of the Lord,' 'my Holy One,' 'my Firstborn' and many others.

"These New Testament writers also taught that the promise of God would operate eternally and irrevocably. Certainly 'a hardening in part' had come over Israel (Rom. 11:25), but nevertheless, 'God's gifts and his call [were] irrevocable' (Rom. 11:29). No less definitive was the announcement from the writer of the book of Hebrews:

> "When God made his promise to Abraham, since there was no one greater for him to swear by, he swore by himself.… Because God wanted to make the unchanging nature of his purpose very clear to the heirs of what was promised, he confirmed it with an oath. God did this so that, by two unchangeable things [his word in Gen. 12 and his oath in Gen. 22] in which it is impossible for God to lie, we [the generations long after Abraham and his immediate heirs] who have fled to take hold of the hope offered to us may be greatly encouraged. (Heb. 6:13, 17–18)

"This promise-plan of God exhibited strong connections with other doctrines throughout the New Testament. God had made it plain to Abraham that the benefits of this promise were not limited to him and his own people alone, but that he and his people were to be a channel through which the same benefits would come to the other nations as well. Paul taught in Galatians 3:6–8 three foundational truths: (1) Abraham received the gospel itself in advance of its fuller and later explication; (2) the substance of this gospel could be found in the words, 'All nations will be blessed through you'; and (3) the gospel was the same one given to Abraham and the one by which all the Gentiles on earth were to be saved at the hearing of the name of Jesus. Paul put it this way: Abraham 'believed God, and it was credited to him as righteousness.' Understand, then, that those who believe are children of Abraham. Scripture foresaw that God would justify the Gentiles by faith, and announced the gospel in advance to Abraham: 'All nations will be blessed through you' (Gal. 3:6–8 NASB).

"Some may wonder why we have not declared as the unifying doctrine of the Bible the theme of 'the kingdom of God,' which Jesus came announcing. But, as Willis J. Beecher, whom we have been following in this presentation, commented: 'The most prominent thing in the New Testament is the proclamation of the kingdom and its anointed king. But it is on the basis of the divine promise that its preachers proclaim the kingdom, and when they appeal to the Old Testament in proof of Christian doctrine, they make the promise more prominent than the kingdom itself.'

"**The time of the arrival of the promise.** John the Baptist, more than any other person, prepared the way for the arrival of the fulfillment of the promise in Jesus the Messiah. John's record is found in all four gospels, amounting to 194 verses, which in its combined total exceeds the total number of verses in seventeen of the twenty-seven books of the New Testament, not to mention seven other allusions to John the Baptist in the book of Acts. John appeared on the scene as abruptly as did his earlier counterpart, Elijah, in 1 Kings 17:1. Despite the fact that there had not been any prophetic or written revelatory material for some four hundred years, suddenly a voice erupted out in the desert calling for men and women to repent and prepare the way of the Lord. Yet all of this should not have been all that surprising, for twice in the promise-plan it had been promised that he and his mission would precede the coming of the one in the Davidic line. John would point to Jesus as the Lamb of God who would take away the sin of the world (John 1:29). Jesus' estimate of John the Baptist would be that he was 'more than a prophet' (Matt. 11:9). In fact, Jesus said, 'Among those born of women there has not risen anyone greater than John the Baptist' (Matt. 11:11).

"Add to John's witness that of Zechariah the priest who, after nine months of speechlessness, broke out in an ecstatic paean of praise to God for keeping his promise to David, to Abraham, and to Zechariah himself, in sending John. Mary, the mother of our Lord, also had a song of praise to God that echoed the song of Hannah, for again God had accomplished what he had promised. Count among this watchful group also the elderly Simeon who, having seen Jesus when Mary and Joseph brought him to the temple for dedication, said that he had seen enough to satisfy him that the fulfillment of the Lord's promise was under way, and now he was ready to depart to be with his Lord. The content of the promise had been the substance of Israel's long-awaited hope."[9]

Record any insights from the brief commentary and quotes:

 ## Think Through the Issues

Again we want to ask the question: Is this Story true? Does it match history? We saw in the Mark passages that Jesus understood that He was the promised King who would come from David's line. In passage after passage we saw that the Scriptures pointed to Jesus just as prophesied—even where He would come from and that He would suffer and die to cover the sins of whoever believed in Him. That was *the gospel*—the good news.

In this section, we will discuss the importance of the good news for our own lives today. We will explore whether this good news announced by Jesus lines up with the unfolding Story of the plan of God in the Jewish Scriptures. We will explore the implications for our lives and whether the Scriptures do point to Jesus as the coming promised king who will set up the promised coming kingdom. We will also explore the implications for our lives as followers of Jesus and this good news, from now until Jesus returns to fully set up the kingdom.

ISSUE: The centrality of the gospel—the good news—for our lives today

Think Through the Issue Before Discussion:

1. In what way does the good news of Jesus Christ fulfill everything promised in the essence of God's plan in the Old Testament Scriptures?
2. Why is it good news for all the families of the earth?
3. As His followers, what, in essence, are we to believe to receive forgiveness of sins and become part of this kingdom?
4. What are implications for His followers now until He returns? What are we to be part of? What are we to be doing now?

Record your initial thoughts on the issue before discussion:

Discuss the issue in your small group.

Record your initial thoughts on the issue after discussion:

 ## Apply the Principles

It is now time to respond to what you have studied and discussed. Take your time on this section.

Think Back Through the First Three Steps.

Design an Application for Your Life.

For several sessions, now, we have been asking whether the Story is true—whether it matches history. Record your growing conviction regarding the validity of the Story. Also, if you conclude it is true, what are the implications for the rest of your life?

THE KINGDOM LAUNCHED 7

In the last session, we saw Jesus announce the good news that the kingdom of God was at hand. God was about to make a major move in His grand strategy. But first, before the launch of this grand strategy, which began with His promise to Abraham to bless all the families of the earth, the promised king from the line of David had to suffer and die. In this section, we will see the launch of this promised kingdom, which would eventually include all the families of the earth. But it is full of surprises. Jesus said He would build His Church, and there is nothing Satan could do to stop it (Matthew 16:18). But no one knew what that meant yet. We will discover these surprises in this session and the next.

I use the term *grand strategy* because it has great historical roots. For example, Rome had a grand strategy—the Roman Empire. The Greek empire had a grand strategy. The Byzantine Empire had a grand strategy. In sessions 7 and 8, we will see God's grand strategy unfold with great power. But we still have to ask, is it true? Did it really happen, and is it still happening today? And should we decide to be a part of it? We will begin with the two books of Luke, designed to show God's grand strategy fully and to call us to be part of it.

Study the Scriptures

READ THE PASSAGES: ACTS 1:1–8; GENESIS 12:1–3

Think Through the Questions:

1. Why do you think Acts 1:1–8 is so important?
2. In what way does Acts 1:8 give shape to the launching of this new kingdom?
3. In what way does this passage help develop the metanarrative established in Genesis 12:1–3?
4. What new elements are added to the Story by this passage?

Summarize the Core Teaching of the Passages:

Summarize what Acts 1:1–8 adds to the promise, and comment on why this passage is so important in understanding the storyline of the Scriptures—the Law, the Prophets, and the Writings. Try to identify the role of this passage in the overall plan set forth in Genesis 12:1–3, which would eventually include all the nations of the earth.

Core teaching of Acts 1:1–8 and Genesis 12:1–3:

Consult the Scholars

The following comments are designed to help you better understand the passage and to stimulate your thinking on the implications of the teaching.

Read and Reflect on this Brief Commentary on Acts 1:1–8 and Genesis 12:1–3:

First, review Appendix A—the Story so far.

We will focus our study on the writings of Luke. Luke wrote 2 volumes: Luke—volume 1 and Acts—volume 2. Luke is shaping the mission, the launching of the kingdom.

> In Luke—His followers are to be witnesses, proclaiming this good news to all the nations, beginning in Jerusalem.
>
> In Acts—He gives more shape to the launching of this kingdom and the mandate to the witnesses.

Let's begin by looking at the structure of the two volumes and Luke's intention in writing these two volumes.

> [1] Since many have undertaken to set down an orderly account of the events that have been fulfilled among us, [2] just as they were handed on to us by those who from the beginning were eyewitnesses and servants of the word, [3] I too decided, after investigating everything carefully from the very first, to write an orderly account for you, most excellent Theophilus, [4] so that you may know the truth concerning the things about which you have been instructed. Luke 1:1–4

> [1] In the first book, Theophilus, I wrote about all that Jesus did and taught from the beginning [2] until the day when he was taken up to heaven, after giving instructions through the Holy Spirit to the apostles whom he had chosen. Acts 1:1–2

Luke tells us what he is doing in his introduction to both volumes. In Luke 1:1–4, we see that Luke wrote an authoritative account ("handed down") of the instructions ("catechism") through the Spirit. In Acts 1:1, we see that he records what Jesus taught and (present tense) continues to teach. Acts was part of the Spirit's instructions Jesus gave. We know, from Jesus' conversation in the upper room with His disciples before His crucifixion (John 16:12–15), He would give His instructions through the Spirit. He gives instructions here, in Acts 1:1–2, through the Spirit and would continue to do so. Those instructions include the plan for the mission that the witnesses are to follow.

Now we turn our attention to the grand strategy. Luke records Jesus' announcing of that grand strategy to the disciples after His resurrection, both at the end of Luke and at the beginning of Acts.

> [44] Then he said to them, "These are my words that I spoke to you while I was still with you—that everything written about me in the law of Moses, the prophets, and the psalms must be fulfilled." [45] Then he opened their minds to understand the scriptures, [46] and he said to them, "Thus it is written, that the Messiah is to suffer and to rise from the dead on the third day, [47] and that repentance and forgiveness of sins is to be proclaimed in his name to all nations, beginning from Jerusalem. [48] You are witnesses of these things. [49] And see, I am sending upon you what my Father promised; so stay here in the city until you have been clothed with power from on high." Luke 24:44–48

> [6] So when they had come together, they asked him, "Lord, is this the time when you will restore the kingdom to Israel?" [7] He replied, "It is not for you to know the times or periods that the Father has set by his own authority. [8] But you will receive power when the Holy Spirit has come upon you; and you will be my witnesses in Jerusalem, in all Judea and Samaria, and to the ends of the earth." Acts 1:6–8

This takes us all the way back to where we started. After opening the minds of the two disciples on the road to Emmaus, He appeared to the rest of the disciples. We see three things here. First, He opens their minds to understand the Scriptures—the Law of Moses, the Prophets, and the Psalms. (This is what we have been studying—our minds are opened.) Second, He reaffirms the good new—the gospel—that the Messiah had to suffer and rise again so that everyone who repents and believes in Him receives forgiveness of sins. And, third, He connects it to all the nations. The disciples are to proclaim this good news to all nations. We now see how all the families of the earth are to be blessed.

In Acts, the commission is made more specific. They are to be witnesses in Jerusalem, in Judea and Samaria, and to the ends of the earth. This is then how Luke structures the book of Acts.

1. The witness in Jerusalem, chs. 1–7

    The disciples waited for the Spirit to come and bring Jesus' instructions in carrying out the work they were called to do. After the Spirit came, Peter gave the good news proclamation, and 3,000 believed. Then the new community of followers devoted themselves to the Apostles' teaching, to fellowship, to breaking of bread, and to prayer (Acts 2:42). This *church* continued to grow in Jerusalem.

2. The witness in Judea and Samaria, chs. 8–12

    Through persecution, after the stoning of Stephen, the church scattered into Judea and Samaria, thus leading to the gospel being proclaimed in that area as well.

3. The witness to the whole world, chs. 13–28

    Then the witness began to spread to the Gentiles, beginning with the church at Antioch. Paul was chosen by God to take the gospel to the Gentiles. We see this begin on Paul's first missionary journey, when he is sent from Antioch to do the work the Spirit called them to do.

Let's pick up the Story in Acts 13, when Paul and Barnabas go to the leaders of the church they helped teach and establish.

> 13:1 Now in the church at Antioch there were prophets and teachers: Barnabas, Simeon who was called Niger, Lucius of Cyrene, Manaen a member of the court of Herod the ruler, and Saul. ² While they were worshiping the Lord and fasting, the Holy Spirit said, "Set apart for me Barnabas and Saul for the work to which I have called them." ³ Then after fasting and praying they laid their hands on them and sent them off. Acts 13:1–3

They were sent out by the leaders to do the work the Spirit told them (Jesus' instructions). What was the work? The Spirit gave specific instructions about the work of being witnesses to all nations. Luke gives shape to that work in Acts 13:1–14:28. It includes at least 3 main elements:

1. They proclaimed the gospel in and around strategic cities.
2. They instructed the new believers—Apostles' teaching.
3. They formed the believers into churches and appointed elders in every church.

We call this work *the Pauline cycle* because Paul follows the same pattern (instructions from the Spirit) on his second and third missionary journeys also. On the second missionary journey, Paul revisits the churches and then follows the same pattern, expanding the witness to new strategic areas. These essential instructions are embedded in the teaching and actions of the Apostles all through Acts, as seen by the shaping "narrative episodes" recorded by Luke and in his shaping summary statements.

> [7] The word of God continued to spread; the number of the disciples increased greatly in Jerusalem, and a great many of the priests became obedient to the faith.
> Acts 6:7

> [31] Meanwhile the church throughout Judea, Galilee, and Samaria had peace and was built up. Living in the fear of the Lord and in the comfort of the Holy Spirit, it increased in numbers.
> Acts 9:31

> [24] But the word of God continued to advance and gain adherents.
> Acts 12:24

> [5] So the churches were strengthened in the faith and increased in numbers daily.
> Acts 16:5

> [20] So the word of the Lord grew mightily and prevailed.   Acts 19:20

> [30] He lived there two whole years at his own expense and welcomed all who came to him, [31] proclaiming the kingdom of God and teaching about the Lord Jesus Christ with all boldness and without hindrance.
> Acts 28:30–31

The word of God continued to advance. The churches continued to multiply.

Now we see the grand strategy unfold. Remember, Acts is "catechetical." It is intended to instruct us in how to carry out the witness. Jesus was giving His instruction in how to carry out the work of being witnesses to the nations—taking the gospel to the nations.

This was to be done by proclaiming the gospel to strategic cites, forming the new believers into churches, and appointing leaders to guard and develop those churches so they would continue to grow and multiply, participating in the continued progress of the gospel.

One final piece of validation. On Paul's first missionary journey, while preaching to the city in Antioch Pisida, Paul, like all the Apostles, validates what is happening from the Jewish Scriptures.

> [44] The next sabbath almost the whole city gathered to hear the word of the Lord. [45] But when the Jews saw the crowds, they were filled with jealousy; and blaspheming, they contradicted what was spoken by Paul. [46] Then both Paul and Barnabas spoke out boldly, saying, "It was necessary that the word of God should be spoken first to you. Since you reject it and judge yourselves to be unworthy of eternal life, we are now turning to the Gentiles. [47] For so the Lord has commanded us, saying,

> 'I have set you to be a light for the Gentiles,
> so that you may bring salvation to the ends of the earth.' " Acts 13:44–47

This is a quote from Isaiah 42, again one of the four "songs of the servant," which all point to Jesus and His death, burial, and resurrection and His following mission of bringing in the kingdom. This song, Isaiah 42, is specifically on His mission. Paul pulls out the heart of the song, to focus on both the mission extending to the Gentles (all nations) and eventually to all of Israel. Jesus is also a "light to the Gentiles" (nations). This drives us back to the Genesis 12:1–3 passage.

Now let's list out these developments together to add to the unfolding Story.

1. Jesus told His disciples that they were to be witnesses in Jerusalem, Judea and Samaria, and to all nations.
2. Jesus told the disciples to go and wait for instructions from the Spirit on how to carry out their witness.
3. They proclaimed the gospel and gathered believers into new communities, formed around the Apostles' teaching.
4. The witness to the nations was given shape through specific work given to Paul and his team.
5. They proclaimed the gospel in and around strategic cities.
6. They instructed the new believers—the Apostles' teaching.
7. They formed the believers into churches and appointed elders in every church.

Now we have the grand strategy framed in. The books of Acts shows us how the kingdom was inaugurated, and gives us a record of Jesus' instructions in how to carry it out until He returns. The surprise is the birth of the Church and its central role in progressing the gospel, through a multiplication of churches, rather than through Israel. Israel consistently rejected God's plan—His grand strategy—as it unfolded in history. In the next session, we will look at that surprise—the Church—in great detail.

Read and Reflect on Key Quotes:

This quote is from N. T. Wright, the most prolific and foremost theologian of Paul in the 20th Century. He continues the tradition of moving from systematic to biblical theology and is "paradigmatically explosive" in his insights regarding Paul and in developing an accurate understanding of the gospel and the kingdom of God, as Christ unfolds His grand strategy through the Church. The remaining three quotes show a growing understanding of the gospel in Paul's writings. They show an understanding of how God's plan for the kingdom is realized through Christ's grand strategy for the Church as the kingdom is inaugurated.

"The first and perhaps most obvious meaning of the resurrection of Jesus, which emerges strongly in all four gospels, is that God has vindicated the Jesus who proclaimed the kingdom and died as Israel's representative. This may sound obvious, but to judge from the reactions I often get when I say this sort of thing I think it is not sufficiently recognized. In Mark's short and probably truncated account there is no sense of 'Jesus is raised, therefore there really is life after death'; rather, the point is, 'Jesus is raised, therefore you'd better go to Galilee and see him there.' For anyone who has read the whole gospel, the strong implication is, 'Jesus is raised, just as he told you he would be; in other words, all that he said about the coming of the kingdom through his own work, through his death and resurrection, has come true.' The resurrection completes the inauguration of God's kingdom. In Mark's perspective, it is at least part of what Jesus meant when he said that some standing with him would not taste death before they saw the kingdom of God come with power. This points us forward to the more detailed outworking in the other gospels. The resurrection is not an isolated supernatural oddity proving how powerful, if apparently arbitrary, God can be when he wants to. Nor is it at all a way of showing that there is indeed a heaven awaiting us after death. It is the decisive event demonstrating that God's kingdom really has been launched on earth as it is in heaven.

"When we turn to Matthew, we find that he takes this further—and it is indeed quite possible that Mark's original text had something like this as well. When the disciples go to Galilee and see Jesus there, they worship him (though some, interestingly, doubt); this is the culmination of the Christology that has been building up throughout the gospel. Jesus is vindicated as the Emmanuel, the man who is God-with-us. But there is no sense either that this is just a nice thing that's happened to him or that the point of it all is for him to say, 'So if you go on behaving yourselves you'll be able to join me in heaven one day.' On the contrary. Just as Jesus taught his followers to pray that God's kingdom would come on earth as in heaven, so now he claims that all authority in heaven and on earth has been given to him, and on that basis he commands the disciples to go and make it happen—to work, in other words, as agents of that authority. What remains implicit in Mark, at least as we have it, is made explicit in Matthew: resurrection doesn't mean *escaping from* the world; it means *mission to* the world based on Jesus's *lordship over* the world.

"Already we begin to see how the watershed works. If the resurrection is an event that actually occurred (in some sense) in time and space as well as in the material reality of Jesus's body, it has implications for other events that must follow. If it's only a so-called spiritual event, either involving Jesus being alive now in some heavenly realm or simply involving a new sense of faith and hope in our minds and hearts, the only events that will follow are various forms of private spirituality. So Matthew gives us the clear message of what the resurrection means: Jesus is now enthroned as the Lord of heaven and earth. His kingdom has been established. And this kingdom is to be put into practice by his followers summoning all nations to obedient allegiance to him, marking them out in baptism. The closing line draws together the major themes of the gospel: the Emmanuel, the God-with-us, is now Jesus-with-us until the final end of the old age, the time when the new age, which has been inaugurated in the resurrection, has completed its transforming work in the world.

"This brings us to Luke, and in particular to the marvelous story of the two disciples on the road to Emmaus. There is much that could be said about Luke 24, but for the moment I simply draw attention to the answer that this chapter gives to the question, So what if Jesus is raised bodily from the dead? The biggest and most important answer is that with the resurrection of Jesus the entire story of God and Israel, and God and the world, must be told in a new way.

"This, again, is watershed stuff. Without the resurrection there is one way of telling the story; with the resurrection there is a whole other way. Without the resurrection, the story is an unfinished and potentially tragic drama in which Israel can hold on to hope but with an increasing sense that the narrative is spinning out of control. Without the resurrection, even the story of Jesus is a tragedy, certainly in first-century Jewish terms, as the two on the road to Emmaus knew very well. But with the resurrection there is a new way of telling the entire story. The resurrection isn't just a surprise happy ending for one person; it is instead the turning point for everything else. It is the point at which all the old promises come true at last: the promises of David's unshakable kingdom; the promises of Israel's return from the greatest exile of them all; and behind that again, quite explicit in Matthew, Luke, and John, the promise that all the nations will now be blessed through the seed of Abraham.

"If Jesus has not been raised, Luke is saying, all you have is hopes raised and dashed once more. The disciples would go on hoping, no doubt, because they were faithful Jews, but if Jesus is not raised, nothing has happened to show that their hopes might after all be fulfilled. But if Jesus has been raised, then this is how the Old Testament has to be read: as a story of suffering and vindication, of exile and restoration, a narrative that reaches its climax not in Israel becoming top nation and beating the rest of the world at its own game but in the suffering and vindication, the exile and restoration, of the Messiah— not for himself alone but because he is carrying the saving promises of God. If the messenger bringing vital news falls into the river and is then rescued, he is rescued not for himself alone but for the sake of those who are waiting in desperate hope for his life-giving message. If Jesus is raised, Luke is saying, he really was and is the Messiah; but if he's the Messiah, he is God's messenger, God's promise-bearer, carrying the promises made to Abraham, Moses, David, and the prophets— promises not only for Israel but also for the whole world.

"That is why, incidentally, the Old Testament must be seen as part of Christian scripture. I respect those who call the Old Testament the Hebrew scriptures to acknowledge that they are still the scriptures of a living faith community different from Christianity. But Luke insists that since Jesus really was raised from the dead, the ancient scriptures of Israel must be read as a story that reaches its climax in Jesus and will then produce its proper fruit not only in Israel but also in Jesus's followers and, through them, in all the world. That's why, when Jesus appears to the disciples in the upper room in verses 36–49, his opening of their minds to understand the scriptures (verses 44–46) results directly in the new commission: that 'repentance and forgiveness of sins is to be proclaimed in his name to all nations, beginning from Jerusalem.' This is not something other than the Jewish hope. It is woven into the scriptures from very early on that when God finally does for Israel what he's going to do, then the nations of the world will come to share in the blessing. This, indeed, is one of the central keys to unlocking New Testament theology.

"Of course, if Jesus is not raised from the dead, we might recognize two sorts of religion or faith: a Christian faith that believed it gained access to the divine through Jesus and a Jewish faith that believed it gained access to the divine apart from Jesus (and was perhaps still waiting for another Messiah). But both of these would be very different from real Christianity and real Judaism. If, out of a desire to be fair to Judaism, you turn both Christianity and Judaism into examples of a religion, a way of ordering your own spirituality, you may be more politically correct, but you will do violence to both actual households of faith. But if Jesus is raised from the dead, then the scriptures have reached their goal in him, and it's now time for the moment the psalmists and prophets longed to see, when the nations of the earth will bring their treasures in loyalty and obedience to God's anointed king, Israel's Messiah.

"The further question, of how Christianity continues to relate to the Judaism that does not recognize Jesus as Messiah, is of course vital. It is addressed in the New Testament, not least by Paul. But we cannot allow our proper sensitivities on this subject to prevent us from speaking of Jesus's resurrection and from embracing the challenge that comes as a result. For Luke, the point of the resurrection is that the long story of Israel, the great overarching scriptural narrative, has reached its goal and climax and must now give birth, as it always intended, to the worldwide mission in which the nations are summoned to turn from their idolatry and find forgiveness of sins. And they are to do this, Luke implies, because in Jesus we see the true God in human form, the reality of which all idols are parodies, and the true forgiveness of sins through his cross, the reality before which all sacrifices are types and shadows. The resurrection, in other words, is for Luke neither an odd miracle that restored Jesus to life but has no other meaning nor a sign that we shall all go to heaven when we die but rather the fulfillment of the ancient scriptural promises and the beginning of God's worldwide mission."[10]

Record any insights from the brief commentary and quotes:

 # Think Through the Issues

In the introduction we talked about God's grand strategy being shaped through Luke's two volumes, Luke and Acts. We saw it unfold in Acts. It is a worldwide multiplication of churches participating in the progress of this good news of Jesus amongst the nations. We ask again, is it true? We talked of the Roman Empire grand strategy. After Acts, what happened? The strategy unfolded, and unfolded, and unfolded within the Roman Empire until it turned the empire upside down. In 312 AD the churches and Christians had multiplied, and the entire empire, under Constantine, actually became the official religion. And God had just begun.

That same strategy is in place today, the progress of the gospel through a worldwide multiplication of churches under apostolic type leaders. As believers, we need to participate in that strategy today. Churches in the 21st century need to follow that strategy today. Most do not. Most have become institutionalized. In this section, we will explore participation in that grand strategy for today. How are we to participate in that grand strategy as followers of Jesus?

ISSUE: Participating in Jesus' grand strategy today

Think Through the Issue Before Discussion:

1. In what way does Acts 1:8 launch the fulfillment of Genesis 12:1–3, by blessing all the families of the earth? In what way is this a launch of the kingdom of God?
2. How is the Church a surprise? How central is the Church (i.e. churches) in that grand strategy?
3. If Luke–Acts is catechetical for us today, how does Acts give shape to our witness today? Are we to do the same work today as the Spirit instructed Paul and Barnabas?
4. What are implications for His followers now until He returns? How are we to participate in that grand strategy?

Record your initial thoughts on the issue before discussion:

Discuss the issue in your small group.

Grasping the Metanarrative in a Postmodern World

Record your initial thoughts on the issue after discussion:

 ## Apply the Principles

It is now time to respond to what you have studied and discussed. Take your time on this section.

Think Back Through the First Three Steps.

Design an Application for Your Life.

Sumarize the essence of Christ's grand strategy for seeing the gospel proclaimed to the ends of the earth, as He launches His kingdom. What does it mean to participate in that strategy today? Reflect on what it means to participate in that strategy and the implications for your own life and ministry.

THE CHURCH AS CHRIST'S GRAND STRATEGY ⑧

Is this Story true? We have been asking that question again and again. Even though previously elements of the Story were completely hidden, in this session we will see that the foundation was actually embedded deeply in the plan of God in the Old Testament. It is often said there are over 300 clear prophesies of Christ in the Old Testament. We will see in Peter's quotes that each of these prophesies is woven carefully into a complex unfolding plan which is so intricate that no one but God could have made this happen.

The Church is the big surprise. It is Christ's grand strategy within God's overall plan. In Christ's plan, the Church will amaze not only the nations but also the rulers and authorities in heavenly places. Often, in reality, this is not the case because churches do not follow Christs strategy, which includes His specific instructions for His churches. In this session, we will examine the more specific instructions within Christ's grand strategy, which we looked at last session. The main passages are Ephesians 2:11–3:13 and 4:1–16. We major on these because they will put Christ's grand strategy into the whole Story and make the direction of our lives as followers of Jesus very clear.

Study the Scriptures

READ THE PASSAGES: KEY TEXT: EPHESIANS 2:11–3:13; 4:1–16; COROLLARY TEXTS: MATTHEW 16:13–20; ACTS 2:42–47; 1 PETER 2:1–10; OLD TESTAMENT VALIDATION TEXTS: ISAIAH 28:16; PSALM 118:22–23

Think Through the Questions:

1. Why do you think Ephesians 2:11–3:13 and 4:1–16 are so important?
2. In what way do they fully reveal the hidden elements of the storyline?
3. In what way do these passages help develop the metanarrative established in Genesis 12:1–3?
4. What new elements are added to the Story by this passage?

Summarize the Core Teaching of the Passages:

Summarize what these passages add to the promise, and comment on why these passages are so important in understanding the storyline of the Scriptures—the Law, the Prophets, and the Writings. Try to identify the role of these passages in the overall plan set forth in Genesis 12:1–3, which would eventually include all the nations of the earth.

Core teaching of Ephesians 2:11–3:13; 4:1–16; Matthew 16:13–20; Acts 2:42–47; 1 Peter 2:1–10; Isaiah 28:16; Psalm 118:22–23:

Consult the Scholars

The following comments are designed to help you better understand the passages and to stimulate your thinking on the implications of the teaching.

Read and Reflect on this Brief Commentary on Ephesians 2:11–3:13; 4:1–16; Matthew 16:13–20; Acts 2:42–47; 1 Peter 2:1–10; Isaiah 28:16; Psalm 118:22–23:

First, review Appendix A—the Story so far.

Last session, we focused on Christ's grand strategy—the Church—and how it is central to the gospel being proclaimed to all the nations. The Church was a surprise. It was not previously revealed. It was a *mystery*—something not revealed before but hidden in the plan of God. The Ephesians passages are our main texts, but let's begin by returning to Acts: 6–8, where the strategy is revealed.

> [6] So when they had come together, they asked him, "Lord, is this the time when you will restore the kingdom to Israel?" [7] He replied, "It is not for you to know the times or periods that the Father has set by his own authority. [8] But you will receive power when the Holy Spirit has come upon you; and you will be my witnesses in Jerusalem, in all Judea and Samaria, and to the ends of the earth." Acts 1:6–8

- The Apostles did as Jesus said and went back and waited for the Spirit to come.
- The Spirit came, as promised, on the day of Pentecost, with a mighty wind.
- People who were gathered from all over the world because of Pentecost, a famous Jewish religious day, heard Peter and others speaking in their own languages.
- Peter delivered a sermon (his first of 5 speeches recorded in Acts, which were in essence the *kerygma*—the proclamation of the gospel story).
- Three thousand believed; a new community was born.

The kingdom was now inaugurated. This newborn community had an extraordinary set of experiences that changed their lives. We get a glimpse of that new community in Acts 2.

> [42] They devoted themselves to the apostles' teaching and fellowship, to the breaking of bread and the prayers. [43] Awe came upon everyone, because many wonders and signs were being done by the apostles. [44] All who believed were together and had all things in common; [45] they would sell their possessions and goods and distribute the proceeds to all, as any had need. [46] Day by day, as they spent much time together in the temple, they broke bread at home and ate their food with glad and generous hearts, [47] praising God and having the goodwill of all the people. And day by day the Lord added to their number those who were being saved. Acts 2:42–47

This new community developed a core identity immediately. It centered around four things, according to Luke.

They devoted themselves to

1. the Apostles' doctrine. This was most likely teaching the kerygma—the proclamation of the gospel—and rooting it in the Scriptures (building on the road to Emmaus).
2. fellowship—koinonia. This was their shared experience in the Spirit: They were the new promised community that was inaugurating the kingdom.
3. the breaking of bread. This refers to eating meals together in homes daily. But

with the definite article in front, it probably refers to elements in those daily meals together that marked them out as a new community following Christ, following the new commandment to love one another (an early version of the Lord's Supper).
4. the Prayers. The new community was taking shape in homes, yet they still observed going to the Temple at 3 p.m. every day for prayer (Acts 3:1; Dunn, *Beginning From Jerusalem*, p. 202).

Several observations are important to make at this time.

- The "sharing in common" was logical because many stayed on after Pentecost and would need food, money, and housing.
- 3,000 believed and were added to this small community of followers who were faithfully waiting for the Spirit.
- Though the term is not used yet, the Church was really birthed at Pentecost, yet the whole understanding of the Church was revealed through Paul. (Acts 5:11 "great fear seized the whole Church.")
- They were still carrying out some of the Jewish practices. They remained devoted to daily prayers in the Temple, which means they still saw themselves as a new community within Judaism.
- They became an incredibly transformed community—enjoying tremendous unity and generously sharing everything in common.

The Apostles did not fully understand what was happening. They knew this was the new community—the Church—that Jesus had said He would build. But most of them thought it was the remnant of Israel, the small group of people within Israel who would believe at the beginning of the kingdom, and then all Israel would follow. They did not fully understand the grand strategy of the Church and why it would become one new community of both Israelites and Gentiles, with a whole new foundation, with Christ as the cornerstone.

That full revelation would come through Paul and his letters to the churches. The main passage is Ephesians 2:11–3:13, followed by Ephesians 4:1–16. Several things are revealed in these passages. First, Paul makes it clear that God has made the Jews and Gentiles one, in a whole new community.

> [19] So then you are no longer strangers and aliens, but you are citizens with the saints and also members of the household of God, [20] built upon the foundation of the apostles and prophets, with Christ Jesus himself as the cornerstone. [21] In him the whole structure is joined together and grows into a holy temple in the Lord; [22] in whom you also are built together spiritually into a dwelling place for God.
>
> Ephesians 2:19–22

A whole new foundation is being laid by Christ's Apostles and prophets, Christ Himself being the cornerstone of that foundation. Paul is given a 2-fold job description. First, he is the one who would preach the gospel to the Gentiles (opening the gospel to them as we saw on his missionary journeys). Second, he is to make clear the mystery.

> ⁷ Of this gospel I have become a servant according to the gift of God's grace that was given me by the working of his power. ⁸ Although I am the very least of all the saints, this grace was given to me to bring to the Gentiles the news of the boundless riches of Christ, ⁹ and to make everyone see what is the plan of the mystery hidden for ages in God who created all things; ¹⁰ so that through the church the wisdom of God in its rich variety might now be made known to the rulers and authorities in the heavenly places. ¹¹ This was in accordance with the eternal purpose that he has carried out in Christ Jesus our Lord, ¹² in whom we have access to God in boldness and confidence through faith in him. ¹³ I pray therefore that you may not lose heart over my sufferings for you; they are your glory.   Ephesians 3:7–13

Paul tells us more about the building of this Church in Ephesians chapter 4.

> ¹¹ The gifts he gave were that some would be apostles, some prophets, some evangelists, some pastors and teachers, ¹² to equip the saints for the work of ministry, for building up the body of Christ, ¹³ until all of us come to the unity of the faith and of the knowledge of the Son of God, to maturity, to the measure of the full stature of Christ. ¹⁴ We must no longer be children, tossed to and fro and blown about by every wind of doctrine, by people's trickery, by their craftiness in deceitful scheming. ¹⁵ But speaking the truth in love, we must grow up in every way into him who is the head, into Christ, ¹⁶ from whom the whole body, joined and knit together by every ligament with which it is equipped, as each part is working properly, promotes the body's growth in building itself up in love.   Ephesians 4:11–16

Paul reveals that the apostolic leaders are to equip the believers to do the work of the ministry, and the whole church will mature in such a way that the world can see Christ in the beauty of the church community.

This is the key passage on understanding that the church is central in the unfolding plan of God. We will just look at the main ideas and how it affects the storyline.

1. Christ's plan—the Church—is a mystery, something not previously revealed (Eph. 3:3 "the mystery was made known to me by revelation"). The word *mystery* pictures something previously hidden.
2. Paul's stewardship is (1) to preach the gospel to the Gentiles and (2) "to bring to light the plan of the mystery"—the mystery being Christ and His plan, which was previously hidden.
3. As a result, the Jews and Gentiles are now one in Christ in His previously hidden plan—the Church.

4. The Church has one foundation, the one laid by the Apostles and prophets, with Jesus as the cornerstone.
5. There is only one foundation: one body, one Spirit, one hope of your calling, one Lord, one faith (one body of teaching), one baptism, one God and Father.
6. The apostles, prophets, evangelists, and pastors and teachers are to build up the church on that one foundation, so that when each one does his or her part, in harmony, people can see Christ in His fullness.
7. Even the rulers and authorities in the heavenly places will be amazed at the wisdom of God through the Church.

A key word in Ephesians 3:10 is the word *plan*—"the plan of the mystery which has been hidden for ages." The word *plan* comes from two words, "house" and the "law"—the house law, administration or plan for the churches. Paul reveals more of that plan in his last three letters: 1 and 2 Timothy and Titus. He tells us this in 1 Timothy 3:

> [14] I hope to come to you soon, but I am writing these instructions to you so that, [15] if I am delayed, you may know how one ought to behave in the household of God, which is the church of the living God, the pillar and bulwark of the truth.
>
> 1 Timothy 3:14,15

We do not have time to study this now, but here are a few things Paul says about Christ's plan for the community life of the churches:

- The churches are to function as a real family—a family of families.
- Older men are to teach younger men; older women younger women.
- Elders are to be trained to lead the churches.
- The churches are to care for the widows.
- Individual families are to be well ordered according to Christ's design.

This idea of a church as a family of families who love and care for each other is at the heart of Christ's plan for His churches. It will be attractive in any culture of the world.

Finally, let's look at Peter and what he says about the Church. We must begin with Christ's statement to Peter, which Peter now understands.

> [13] Now when Jesus came into the district of Caesarea Philippi, he asked his disciples, "Who do people say that the Son of Man is?" [14] And they said, "Some say John the Baptist, but others Elijah, and still others Jeremiah or one of the prophets." [15] He said to them, "But who do you say that I am?" [16] Simon Peter answered, "You are the Messiah, the Son of the living God." [17] And Jesus answered him, "Blessed are you, Simon son of Jonah! For flesh and blood has not revealed this to you, but my Father in heaven. [18] And I tell you, you are Peter, and on this rock I will build my church, and the gates of Hades will not prevail against it. Matthew 16:13–18

This is an important passage describing this new community—the Church—that was to come. Let's make several observations:

- Jesus said He was going to build His Church—a clear statement that a new community was being built.
- It required a whole new foundation. Peter was key to that foundation, but not the cornerstone; that is Christ.
- But Peter would have a foundational role (a small stone). And the statement that "Jesus is the Christ" is the rock upon which it is built.
- Peter will have great authority as it unfolds (to "bind" and to "loose").
- All of Satan and his forces will not be able to stop this Church.

In Peter's first letter to the Jewish churches, he gives us a beautiful passage in 1 Peter 2:1–10. Peter gives us another snapshot of this new Church, rooting the cornerstone—the foundation—in the Old Testament Scriptures.

- Each person is a living stone in this new community of God, the Church.
- The Church is a spiritual house, and each is to worship God through his or her service in this new house.
- The cornerstone of this new spiritual house is Jesus, as predicted in the Old Testament. He is the promised coming king of God's new kingdom.
- The Church is now God's people, designed to proclaim the excellencies of God, who called each person out of darkness into light.

In building his case, Peter draws on the Old Testament, showing that the cornerstone of this new plan, fully revealed by Paul, was deeply rooted in Old Testament prophecy. He draws on three passages:

Psalm 118—a song of thanksgiving (a royal psalm).

Isaiah 28—a chapter in a section judging corrupt rulers, priests, and prophets in Israel.

Isaiah 8—a chapter in the section of Isaiah chapters 7–11, which is full of predictions of this coming King.

In each of the following passages, Peter shows us his whole rethinking of the Scriptures. His mind has truly been opened to understanding the Scriptures. The first is Psalms 118.

> [22] The stone that the builders rejected
> has become the chief cornerstone.
> [23] This is the Lord's doing;
> it is marvelous in our eyes.   Psalm 118:22–23

Let's examine the context from which Peter drew this Old Testament quote:

- It is referred to as a psalm of victory, actually a song of individual thanksgiving (also called a royal psalm).
- The focus is David praising the Lord for victory; the focus is lovingkindness (*hesed*)—God's everlasting love.
- The specific reference to "the chief cornerstone" is of David, as his kingdom is established.

- Peter (and I think David) saw this as a "generic prophecy," as Kaiser calls it, which is sort of an early installment of what was to come, from the king coming from his line—the chief cornerstone.

In Peter's second quote, Isaiah 28:13–16 is used perfectly in the context of the Church understanding its identity in the hidden plan of God.

- The context of Isaiah 28 is judgment on corrupt rulers, priests, and prophets.
- When these leaders needed to be giving rest to the people, they instead created an exacting legalistic system ("line by line").
- God will judge them by their same rules.
- Yet God is laying a whole new foundation. The cornerstone is a tested ruler, who will lay a whole new foundation.

Good choice Peter! In the third passage, Isaiah 8:14, Peter continues to make his case for the Church being the fulfillment of God's unfolding promise. Several observations:

- Context: Chapter 8 sets up Isaiah 9:1–7.
- Both houses of Israel will stumble—all Israel.
- God will save a remnant of Israel from every nation where they are scattered.
- The Stone ("born of a virgin," 7:14; "from Galilee," 9:1; "the root of Jesse," 11:1) will set up His kingdom.

Peter knew where to go in the Scriptures. He had now rethought everything in the Old Testament, and this part of Isaiah became alive to him. To see the amazing predictions of even the hidden plan of the Church is a tremendous apologetic for the truth of this whole Story.

Now let's put the whole picture together, which shows us the details of Christ's master strategy.

1. Christ's plan—the Church—is a mystery, something hidden, not previously revealed (Eph. 3:3 "the mystery was made known to me by revelation").
2. Paul's stewardship was (1) to preach the gospel to the Gentiles and (2) "to bring to light the plan of the mystery"—the mystery being Christ and His plan, previously hidden.
3. Paul also revealed Christ's specific strategy for the community life of His churches. A church is a family of families, which by its community life will show the beauty of Christ.
4. As a result, Jews and Gentiles are now one in Christ in the Church, which was God's previously hidden plan.
5. The Church has one foundation: the one laid by the Apostles and prophets, with Jesus as the cornerstone.

6. There is only one foundation: one body, one Spirit, one hope of your calling, one Lord, one faith (one body of teaching), one baptism, one God and Father.

7. Apostles, prophets, evangelists, and pastors and teachers are to build up the Church on that one foundation. Then, when each one is doing his or her part, in harmony, people can see Christ in His fullness.

8. Even the rulers and authorities in the heavenly places will be amazed at the wisdom of God through the Church.

9. Jesus predicted He would build His church, and nothing of Satan and this world could stop it.

10. Though it was Paul's job to fully bring to light Christ's plan through His Church, Peter rooted its foundation in the prophecies of the Old Testament: Jesus is the cornerstone of this new global people, the Church.

Read and Reflect on Key Quotes:

This is the second of three quotes from N. T. Wright. This one is taken from his book *Pauline Perspectives: Essays on Paul, 1978–2013*. These quotes form a growing understanding of the gospel in Paul's writings and an understanding of how God's plan for the kingdom is realized through Christ's grand strategy for the Church as the kingdom is inaugurated.

"The Central Symbol: The United Family
When you go to the shelves and pick off a volume on Pauline theology, the chances are there will be a chapter on 'the church', but it will probably come some way towards the back of the book. When the writer has exhausted the topics of God, humans, sin, salvation, Jesus Christ and his death and resurrection, the Spirit and so on—finally they may get to a chapter on the church. And within that, as one subsection among many, you will find, perhaps, 'the unity of the church', with an exploration of Paul's different metaphors, the body of Christ, the new Temple and so on. I think that is just the projection onto Paul of certain types of Western Protestant thinking. When we read Paul in his own terms, we find that for him the one, single community is absolutely central. The community of Christ, in Christ, by the Spirit, is at the very heart of it all.

"I love the doctrine of justification. It is hugely important. But it only really occurs in Romans and Galatians, with little flickers elsewhere. But wherever you look in Paul, you see him arguing for, and passionately working for, the unity of the church. We've seen it, close up and personal, in Philemon. In Galatians, the real thrust of the whole letter is that Jewish Christians and gentile Christians should sit at the same table together. That's not incidental; it's the main point of the argument. And in 1 Corinthians, of course, the unity of the church is one of the main themes of the letter, all through, not just in chapter 12. 'Is Christ divided? Of course not.' The exposition builds all the way to the picture of the single body with many members in chapter 12. And then, in case you wondered how that could happen, Paul writes that majestic poem on agapĒ, love. Then, in 1 Corinthians 14, we see what that must look like in the worshiping life of the church; God is not the God of chaos, but of order. And then, in chapter 15, all of this is rooted in the gospel which speaks of new creation, of the kingdom of God, because of the resurrection of Jesus himself from the dead.

"Then, in Philippians, the question is raised: how are you going to 'let your public life be worthy of the gospel of Christ' (Philippians 1.27)? Answer, in chapter 2: 'make my joy complete by being of the same mind, having the same love, being in full accord and of one mind' (verse 2). Have you ever tried that, in a group of three or four? Have you ever tried it in a group of fifteen or twenty? In a group of a thousand or more? It is very, very difficult. Don't imagine it was any easier in the first century. But don't imagine that just because we all find it difficult we can go soft on this central imperative. Rather, recognize that the only way to do it is through what Paul says next.

"Let this mind be in you, which you have in the Messiah, Jesus: he was in the form of God, but didn't regard his equality with God as something to exploit, but emptied himself, becoming obedient to death, even the death of the cross. Therefore God highly exalted him, and bestowed on him the name above every name, that at the name of Jesus every knee should bow, and every tongue confess Jesus Christ as Lord, to the glory of God the father. (Philippians 2.5–11)

"There's the secret, the living heart of this new, revolutionary way of being human. That's why Paul can at once go on to urge: 'do all things without grumbling or questioning, so that you may be blameless and innocent, children of God without blemish in a dark world among whom you shine like lights' (Philippians 2.14–15). You see the point: the unity of the church, the new way of humble unity lived out by the followers of Jesus, is to be the sign to the church that there is a different way of being human.

"Or one could consider the letter to the Ephesians. The unity of Jew and gentile in Christ (2.11–21) is the direct outflowing of that exposition of justification in 2.1–10. And then in chapter 3 this explodes in the glorious truth that through the church, the multicoloured, many-tongued family, the manifold wisdom of God might be made known to the principalities and powers in the heavenly places. It is the fact of a new family that declares to Caesar that he doesn't run the show any more, because Jesus Christ runs it instead. It is the fact of a new, single, united family that tells the powers of the world that Israel's God is God, that Jesus is Lord and Caesar is not. As long as we continue to collude with things that no Paulinist should ever collude with—fragmentation, petty squabbles, divisions over this or that small point of doctrine—the powers can fold their arms and watch us having our little fun while they really still run the show. But when there actually is one body, one spirit, one hope, one Lord, one faith, one baptism (Ephesians 4), then the powers are called to account, and they will know it. Something new has happened, and the gates of hell shall not shall prevail against it.

"And there's a cost; the cost of being different. That's why we have the challenge of marriage in Ephesians 5, in which the coming together of male and female—and what a challenge that always has been, and still is—symbolizes once more the coming together of Jew and gentile, which symbolizes again the coming together of heaven and earth. That is why it's so important that in our generation we struggle again for the sanctity and vitality of marriage, not for the sake of maintaining a few outmoded ethical concepts and taboos but because this is built deep into creation itself, now to be renewed in Christ and the Spirit.

"Then consider the ecumenical imperative in Romans itself. Many of you have lectured or preached on Romans, and you will know what happens. You have the schedule organized; you know how you want it to go, and somehow the exposition of the first eight chapters eats up the time allotted for chapters 9–11, and then when you've dealt with those chapters in turn you hardly have any time left for chapters 12–16. But actually in chapters 14–15 we have some of the most profound teaching anywhere in scripture on the unity of the church and how to maintain it. It isn't a detached topic; it grows directly out of all that has gone before in this most majestic of letters. The hard-won, complex unity of the church, which results in the church glorifying the God and father of our Lord Jesus Christ with one heart and voice: that's what it's all about. 15.7–13 is the climax of the theological exposition of the whole letter, and it insists on the united worship of the multi-cultural church as the ultimate aim of the gospel. That is the heart of Paul's ecclesiology.11

Record any insights from the brief commentary and quotes:

Think Through the Issues

The Church is an amazing grand strategy. According to Paul, it will amaze the world and even the rulers and authorities in heavenly places, if Jesus' instructions are followed. Sadly, today, most churches have been institutionalized and fail to follow Christ's grand strategy. If followed, it is amazing. It works in every culture in every century. The gospel is progressing around the world in the Global South (Latin America, Africa, and Asia: India, SE Asia, Indonesia, and China) much like the Early Church. It is declining in the secular West. Both need to fully understand Christ's grand strategy to participate fully.

In the last session, we saw the framework of Christ's grand strategy. Building on that framework, in this session, we looked at that strategy more in-depth—the Church, and Christ's plan for building it. In this section, we want to explore what it means to shape our lives, our families, and our churches around that strategy. For many in the West, that means very significant renewal around Christ's strategy and instructions for His churches. For those in the global South, it means fully grasping His strategy and instructions for His churches at a time when the Spirit is moving in major ways. Remember, His Spirit works consistent with Christ's grand strategy and instructions for the churches. We cannot ignore them and expect to turn the world upside down as did the Early Church.

ISSUE: The Church as the center of Jesus' grand strategy

Think Through the Issue Before Discussion:

1. In what way is the Church the center of Christ's grand strategy?

2. What is our responsibility as members of this new people of God—the Church—both collectively and individually?

3. How do we know if we are properly lined up with this new plan?

4. What doees it mean to both follow Christ's grand strategy and shape our lives, families, and churches around that plan?

Record your initial thoughts on the issue before discussion:

Discuss the issue in your small group.

Record your initial thoughts on the issue after discussion:

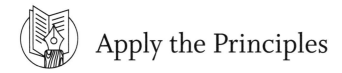# Apply the Principles

It is now time to respond to what you have studied and discussed. Take your time on this section.

Think Back Through the First Three Steps.

Design an Application for Your Life.

Summarize the centrality of the Church as the heart of Christ's grand strategy. What are the implications for our churches and for our own lives—even the shape of our family life and the stewardship of our gifts, time, and resources.

THE KINGDOM FULLY REALIZED 9

Now we come to our final session. Remember the last part of the kerygma statement is that Jesus will return as king and judge. In this session, we will look at the global situation preceding that return. We will keep asking the question of whether this whole metanarrative, this grand strategy, is true. We have said all along that if it is true, then it must match the unfolding history. We will grapple with the key passages around the return of Christ and attempt to frame in the world situation leading to His return.

In addition, we will look at the future of Israel, the nation God built to represent Himself to the nations. Now, the Church, one new people made up of Jews and Gentiles, is to proclaim God's good news. While it is obvious that the nation is no longer in the position of representing God to the world and never will be again, God will not forget His promises to His nation. But what will that look like? How does that fit into this unfolding grand strategy? We will build a framework for these answers in this section.

Study the Scriptures

READ THE PASSAGES: KEY TEXT: MATTHEW 23:37–24:31 COROLLARY TEXTS: ACTS 1:1–11; ROMANS 9:1–8, 30–33; 10:1–4; 11:25–27 OLD TESTAMENT VALIDATION TEXTS: ZECHARIAH 14:1–9

Think Through the Questions:

1. Why do you think Matthew 23:37–24:31 is so important?
2. How should this passage shape our understanding of world events?
3. In what way does this passage help develop the metanarrative established in Genesis 12:1–3?
4. What new elements are added to the Story by this passage?

Summarize the Core Teaching of the Passages:

Summarize what these passages add to the promise, and comment on why these passages are so important in understanding the storyline of the Scriptures—the Law, the Prophets, and the Writings. Try to identify the role of these passages in the overall plan set forth in Genesis 12:1–3, which would eventually include all the nations of the earth.

Core teaching of Matthew 23:37–24:31; Acts 1:1–11; Romans 9:1–8, 30–33; 10:1–4; 11:25–27; Zechariah 14:1–9:

Consult the Scholars

The following comments are designed to help you better understand the passages and to stimulate your thinking on the implications of the teaching.

Read and Reflect on this Brief Commentary on Matthew 23:37–24:31; Acts 1:1–11; Romans 9:1–8, 30–33; 10:1–4; 11:25–27; Zechariah 14:1–9

First, review Appendix A—the Story so far.

We want to begin by returning to the scene in Acts 1:1–12, of Jesus with His disciples just before He ascended to heaven. The disciples are asking if He is going to set up the kingdom of Israel now? He tells them not to worry about that but to just focus on proclaiming His kingdom to the nations, beginning in Jerusalem. Jesus then ascends to heaven, and two men in white promise He will return just as He left. Then the disciples leave the Mount of Olives and return to Jerusalem to wait for the Spirit to come with Jesus' instructions. We now want to examine the world situation and circumstances around His return.

Two important observations need to be made at this time:

1. The disciples ask when He is going restore the kingdom. They mean in this context, "Are you fully setting up the promised kingdom?" He tells them it is not for them to know; they are just to focus on being witnesses to the whole world.

2. Jesus will return just as He left, according to the two men in white robes. This establishes the return of Christ at a future date, to fully set up the kingdom. Jesus had already promised His return, Matthew 24:1–31.

A little earlier (in Matthew 24), they basically asked Jesus the same question, just after Jesus predicted (in Matthew 23:37–39) that their house would be desolate until He returns. Then He predicts the destruction of the temple, implying the destruction of Jerusalem. They asked Him later, sitting on the Mount of Olives (again symbolic of His return), when will these things happen and what will be the sign of Your coming? This is the essence of His answer (in Matthew 24:4–31):

1. Israel's house (as promised through the line of David) will be left desolate until Christ returns, since He is the promised king from the line of David.

2. Israel will undergo an era of being hated by all nations and, by implication, the new people, the Church, will be hated by all nations.

3. Before the end comes and the kingdom is fully realized, there will be a great increase of wars (nation against nation) and an increase of natural catastrophes.

4. Jerusalem will be destroyed (70 AD) and Israel will be scattered around the world. A future hatred of Israel will be led by a world leader (predicted in Daniel) who would destroy Israel, were it not for the return of Christ.

5. Christ's return will not be until the good news of the kingdom (the gospel, the kerygma) is proclaimed to the whole world.

6. When Christ returns, He will gather His people—His kingdom—from all peoples of the world and fully inaugurate His kingdom.

7. The Church's job, as stated in Luke 24 and Acts 1, is to proclaim the gospel to the whole world until the return of Christ.

In both of these passages, the Mount of Olives is key. He ascends to heaven from the Mount of Olives, and He predicts the future of His return while sitting on the Mount of Olives. Let's go back to the Jewish Scriptures in Zechariah the prophet and look at his prediction.

> 14:1 See, a day is coming for the Lord, when the plunder taken from you will be divided in your midst. ² For I will gather all the nations against Jerusalem to battle, and the city shall be taken and the houses looted and the women raped; half the city shall go into exile, but the rest of the people shall not be cut off from the city. ³ Then the Lord will go forth and fight against those nations as when he fights on a day of battle. ⁴ On that day his feet shall stand on the Mount of Olives, which lies before Jerusalem on the east; and the Mount of Olives shall be split in two from east to west by a very wide valley; so that one half of the Mount shall withdraw northward, and the other half southward. ⁵ And you shall flee by the valley of the Lord's mountain, for the valley between the mountains shall reach to Azal; and you shall flee as you fled from the earthquake in the days of King Uzziah of Judah. Then the Lord my God will come, and all the holy ones with him. ⁶ On that day there shall not be either cold or frost. ⁷ And there shall be continuous day (it is known to the Lord), not day and not night, for at evening time there shall be light. ⁸ On that day living waters shall flow out from Jerusalem, half of them to the eastern sea and half of them to the western sea; it shall continue in summer as in winter. ⁹ And the Lord will become king over all the earth; on that day the Lord will be one and his name one.
>
> Zechariah 14:1–9

The prophecy exactly matches Jesus' conversation with the disciples on the Mount of Olives:

1. In the day of Christ's return, He will gather all nations to a great battle against Israel.
2. Christ will then return and defeat the nations in a great battle and fully establish His kingdom.
3. Jerusalem will be the center of this kingdom, and He will be king over all the earth, and everyone will know who He is.
4. His kingdom will bring life to all nations—living water.

The same images are used in John's Revelation when describing the end battles and the kingdom rule of Christ.

> 21:1 Then I saw a new heaven and a new earth; for the first heaven and the first earth had passed away, and the sea was no more. ² And I saw the holy city, the new Jerusalem, coming down out of heaven from God, prepared as a bride adorned for her husband....
>
> 22:1 Then the angel showed me the river of the water of life, bright as crystal, flowing from the throne of God and of the Lamb ² through the middle of the street of the city. On either side of the river is the tree of life with its twelve kinds of fruit, producing its fruit each month; and the leaves of the tree are for the healing of the nations. ³ Nothing accursed will be found there any more. But the throne of God and of the Lamb will be in it, and his servants will worship him; ⁴ they will see his face, and his name will be on their foreheads. ⁵ And there will be no more night; they

need no light of lamp or sun, for the Lord God will be their light, and they will reign forever and ever.

There is not time for it here, but in the book of Revelation, the 7 churches of John are given a glimpse of what will happen when He returns and after His return.

1. The revelation is given to the seven churches, a network John worked amongst near the end of his life. (Revelation 1–3)

2. The battle is given in detail and will take seven years. Babylon, a city that symbolizes the nations as a whole and their resistance to God and His plan, will be defeated. (Revelation 4–18)

3. Jesus will rule for 1,000 years in the promised kingdom. At the end of that time, God will reshape the heavens and the earth, and Christ will rule forever from a New Jerusalem—the Lamb and His bride. (Revelation 19–21)

So what about the nation of Israel? They rejected Christ and, for the most part, still do. Since the Jews and Gentiles who believe are now one new people in the Church, which is the emerging kingdom inaugurated at Pentecost, some say there is no future for Israel. But that is not Paul's view. It is not consistent with important elements of the Story. Here are a few excerpts from Romans 9–11, which help resolve this tension:

> 9:1 I am speaking the truth in Christ—I am not lying; my conscience confirms it by the Holy Spirit—² I have great sorrow and unceasing anguish in my heart. ³ For I could wish that I myself were accursed and cut off from Christ for the sake of my own people, my kindred according to the flesh. ⁴ They are Israelites, and to them belong the adoption, the glory, the covenants, the giving of the law, the worship, and the promises; ⁵ to them belong the patriarchs, and from them, according to the flesh, comes the Messiah, who is over all, God blessed forever. Amen. ⁶ It is not as though the word of God had failed. For not all Israelites truly belong to Israel, ⁷ and not all of Abraham's children are his true descendants; but "It is through Isaac that descendants shall be named for you." ⁸ This means that it is not the children of the flesh who are the children of God, but the children of the promise are counted as descendants. Romans 9:1–8

> ³⁰ What then are we to say? Gentiles, who did not strive for righteousness, have attained it, that is, righteousness through faith; ³¹ but Israel, who did strive for the righteousness that is based on the law, did not succeed in fulfilling that law. ³² Why not? Because they did not strive for it on the basis of faith, but as if it were based on works. They have stumbled over the stumbling stone, ³³ as it is written, "See, I am laying in Zion a stone that will make people stumble, a rock that will make them fall, and whoever believes in him will not be put to shame." Romans 9:30–33

> 10:1 Brothers and sisters, my heart's desire and prayer to God for them is that they may be saved. ² I can testify that they have a zeal for God, but it is not enlightened. ³ For, being ignorant of the righteousness that comes from God, and seeking to

establish their own, they have not submitted to God's righteousness. [4] For Christ is the end of the law so that there may be righteousness for everyone who believes.

Romans 10:1–4

[25] So that you may not claim to be wiser than you are, brothers and sisters, I want you to understand this mystery: a hardening has come upon part of Israel, until the full number of the Gentiles has come in. [26] And so all Israel will be saved; as it is written,

"Out of Zion will come the Deliverer;
he will banish ungodliness from Jacob."
[27] "And this is my covenant with them,
when I take away their sins."

Romans 11:25–27

The essence of Paul's argument on the future of Israel is this:

1. Not all Israelites belong to Israel. Though they are heirs of all the promises, only those who have faith in God through the promises belong to Israel (saved by faith not flesh).

2. Israel has zeal but has not been enlightened. A partial hardening has come over the nations until all the Gentiles are brought into the kingdom, then Israel as a whole will respond. Therefore, we as Gentiles should not be arrogant, but we should enlighten ourselves as to God's enduring promises to Israel.

3. Whereas just a few from the nation of Israel believed at the inauguration of the kingdom in early Acts, the nation as a whole (not everyone) will respond and believe at the return of Christ.

Final observations on Israel:

1. Israel is no longer the tool God is using to proclaim the kingdom to the nations; it is the Church. The Church has replaced the nation of Israel as God's people.

2. It took a long time for the Jewish churches to understand that they were not part of a remnant that would restore Israel, but they were part of a whole new people—the Church, made up of both Jews and Gentiles.

3. God will fulfill His promises to Israel—He will return and destroy the nations that gather to destroy Israel, and most of Israel will believe at that time and become true "Jews" and part of the Church.

Now let's put it all together so we get a picture of the future return of Christ and full realization of the kingdom, thus completing the storyline.

The Plan for the History of Mankind (developed further)

1. Israel's house (as promised through the line of David) will be left desolate until Christ returns, since He is the promised king from the line of David. Israel will

undergo an era of being hated by all nations, filled with many false messiahs.

2. Before the end comes and the kingdom is fully realized, there will be a great increase of wars (nation against nation) and an increase of natural catastrophes. A final hatred of Israel will culminate, led by a world leader (predicted by Daniel) who would destroy Israel were it not for the return of Christ. The Church, God's new people, will be persecuted and hated by the nations as well.

3. In the day of Christ's return, He will gather all nations to a battle against Israel. Christ will then return and defeat the nations in a great battle and fully establish His kingdom. Jerusalem will be the center of this kingdom. Christ will be king over all the earth, and everyone will know who He is.

4. Not all Israelites belong to Israel. Though they are heirs of all the promises, only those who have faith in God through the promises belong to Israel (saved by faith not flesh). Israel has zeal but has not been enlightened.

5. A partial hardening has come over the nations until all the Gentiles are brought into the kingdom; then Israel as a whole will respond. Therefore, we as Gentiles should not be arrogant, but we should enlighten ourselves as to God's enduring promises to Israel. Whereas just a few from the nation of Israel believed at the inauguration of the kingdom in early Acts, the nation as a whole (not everyone) will respond and believe at the return of Christ.

6. The return will not be until the good news of the kingdom (the gospel, the kerygma) is proclaimed to the whole world. When Christ returns, He will gather His people—His kingdom—from all peoples of the world and fully inaugurate His kingdom. Our job is to proclaim the gospel to the whole world until the return of Christ.

Once again, we need to come back to the issue we started with: Is this whole Story true? We have been asking you to consider its truth along the way. We live in a powerful time in history that allows us to see how the world is shaping up, and we must hold that up to the Scriptures. It may not continue to unfold this way, but currently it is amazing.

This area of Israel's history is where it all began and where it will all end before the kingdom is set up.

Walk-through map (Tigris, Euphrates, Fertile Crescent, Babylon, etc.)

Many believe the Garden of Eden was in the Fertile Crescent area.

Abraham journeyed from Ur to Haran—the length of the Euphrates.

Babylon is the heart of the opposition of the nations in Genesis and Revelation. (BDAG—Bauer, Danker, Arndt, and Gingrich, A Greed-English Lexicon of the New Testament (University of Chicato Press 2000.)

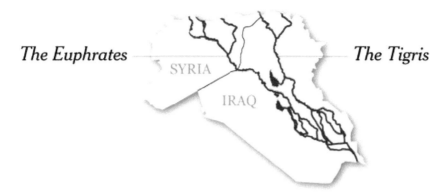

The Euphrates — *The Tigris*
SYRIA
IRAQ

Recently, there was an amazing article in the *New York Times* newspaper that showed how the world is unfolding in the Middle East today. Here is a quote from that article: "A Rogue State Along Two Rivers: How ISIS Came to Control Large Portions of Syria and Iraq," by Jeremy Ashkenas, Archie Tse, Derek Watkins, and Karen Yourish, July 3, 2014, *New York Times:*

> "The militant group called the Islamic State in Iraq and Syria, or ISIS, seemed to surprise many American and Iraqi officials with the recent gains it made in its violent campaign to create a new religious state. But the rapid-fire victories achieved over a few weeks in June were built on months of maneuvering along the Tigris and Euphrates Rivers.
>
> "After establishing footholds in Syria and Anbar Province, ISIS turned to northern Iraq. The swift capture of Mosul, Iraq's second-largest city and a key political, military and commercial hub, gave ISIS a launching pad for a rapid series of attacks in which its fighters seized towns along the Tigris River heading south to Baghdad."

This is ISIS' goal, and at the heart of it is a hatred toward Israel and the West and the driving of Christians out of the Middle East. This globe shows their footprint and Middle East cells.

How ISIS expands:
1. Controlling and governing
2. Infiltrating communities
3. Absorbing other groups

It wants to drive out all Christians and destroy Israel.

And the world's attitude toward Israel is growing worse. Read this quote from "BBC Poll: International Attitudes Toward Israel on Downward Trajectory" by Richard Silverstein on May 18, 2012, in *Mideast Peace*.

> "There is only one country in the world where views of Israel have become more favorable…you guessed it: the U.S. Thanks to MFA hasbara efforts and the unrelenting pressure of the Israel lobby, perceptions of Israel here have improved and are now at the highest level (50% positive) since tracking began in 2005.
>
> "The U.S. is not an island in the world, impermeable and inattentive to attitudes on the rest of the globe. The overwhelming negativity toward Israel will catch up here in the U.S. Take a look at some of the results: Spain—74% negative, up 8 points since 2011, France—65%, up 9 points, German and Britain—69% and 68% respectively, Australia—65%, up 7%, Canada—59% up 7%, South Korea—69%, up 15 points."

In what ways should this part of the Story be part of our proclamation? How does this affect your confidence in the Story? Since the kingdom has been inaugurated and we are at the heart of that kingdom, how should we live in it? How should we view the world we live in? It is a difficult tension to keep in balance. On the one hand, Christ has inaugurated His kingdom, and He is building His Church at the heart of it. The nations will resist Him and thus the world will always be following a plan opposite it.

Let me use a quote from N. T. Wright's *Surprised by Hope*, in which he addresses the issue of the world building its kingdom and Christ building His, in the same location—the radical challenge His kingdom set before our world. This is from chapter nine, "Jesus, The Coming Judge."

> "The ascension and appearing of Jesus constitute a radical challenge to the entire thought structure of the Enlightenment (and of course several other movements)."

In his new book *Simply Good News: Why the Gospel is News and What Makes It Good*, he continues exploring this tension. This quote is from chapter 6, "Wrong Future, Wrong Present." Speaking of the Enlightenment thought structure of man's progress toward a perfect society, he states,

> "You might have thought that two world wars, the Gulag and Auschwitz, stock market crashes, famines and tribal conflict in Africa, the desperate plight of the Balkans, and the recent atrocities of violent fundamentalists would make people pause, scratch their heads, and wonder whether progress is still on track. That doesn't seem to happen."

What should our thought structure, worldview, and belief framework look like?

Part 1

> God's plan: worldwide progress of the gospel through the multiplication of churches. As churches become established and their families and believers mature, the churches (and believers) are to engage in good occupations and to meet pressing needs.

Part 2

> Nations (not necessarily cities, individuals, and sometimes nations) are going to hate Israel and eventually gather together to destroy it.
>
> Nations (not necessarily cities, individuals, and sometimes nations) are going to hate the Church (and Christians) and eventually gather together to destroy it.

Al-Qaeda/ISIS has a very well developed complex network under development. It is Satan's imitation of Christ's grand strategy for the Church. See my two encyclical small books: *The Churches of the First Century: From Simple Churches to Complex Networks*, and *Kerygmatic Communities: Evangelism and the Early Churches*.

Read and Reflect on Key Quotes:

This is the final quote from N. T. Wright. We've looked at three quotes from him to gain insight on Paul's growing understanding of what was happening as the kingdom was being inaugurated. Paul and the Apostles had to fully understand the gospel and realize how God's plan for the kingdom was being realized through Christ's grand strategy for the Church. This quote taken from *Surprised by Hope* looks at what really is the kingdom of God!

"THE KINGDOM OF GOD
We have seen at several points in this book that the normal Christian understanding of kingdom, especially of kingdom of heaven, is simply mistaken. 'God's kingdom' and 'kingdom of heaven' mean the same thing: the sovereign rule of God (that is, the rule of heaven, of the one who lives in heaven), which according to Jesus was and is breaking in to the present world, to earth. That is what Jesus taught us to pray for. We have no right to omit that clause from the Lord's Prayer or to suppose that it doesn't really mean what it says.

"This, as we have seen, is what the resurrection and ascension of Jesus and the gift of the Spirit are all about. They are designed not to take us away from this earth but rather to make us agents of the transformation of this earth, anticipating the day when, as we are promised, 'the earth shall be full of the knowledge of the Lord, as the waters cover the sea.' When the risen Jesus appears to his followers at the end of Matthew's gospel, he declares that all authority in heaven *and on earth* has been given to him. When John the Seer hears the thundering voices in heaven, they are singing, 'The kingdom of the world has become the kingdom of our Lord and of his Messiah, and he shall reign forever and ever.' And the point of the gospels—of Matthew, Mark, Luke, and John together with Acts—is that *this has already begun.*

"The question of *how* it has begun—in what sense it is inaugurated, anticipated, or whatever— has been the stuff of debate for a long time. But part of the problem with that debate is that those taking part in it do not usually clarify the question of *what precisely it is* that is begun, launched, or initiated. At one level it is clearly the hope of Israel, as expressed in classic kingdom passages such as Isaiah 52: 7–12. There, 'God becoming king at last' means the end of exile, the defeat of evil, and the return of Israel's God to Zion. We can see all of that becoming the major theme not only of Jesus's life and public career but also of his own interpretation of his death.

"But underneath that again, when we stand back, is the meaning of God's kingdom, to which the hope of Israel was designed to contribute—or, to put it another way, the meaning because of which God called Israel in the first place. Faced with his beautiful and powerful creation in rebellion, God longed to set it right, to rescue it from continuing corruption and impending chaos and to bring it back into order and fruitfulness. God longed, in other words, to reestablish his wise sovereignty over the whole creation, which would mean a great act of healing and rescue. He did not want to rescue humans *from* creation any more than he wanted to rescue Israel *from* the Gentiles. He wanted to rescue Israel *in order that Israel might be a light to the Gentiles,* and he wanted thereby to rescue humans *in order that humans might be his rescuing stewards over creation.* That is the inner dynamic of the kingdom of God.

"That, in other words, is how the God who made humans to be his stewards over creation and who called Israel to be the light of the world is to become king, in accordance with his original intention in creation, on the one hand, and his original intention in the covenant, on the other. To snatch saved souls away to a disembodied heaven would destroy the whole point. God is to become king of the whole world at last. And he will do this not by declaring that the inner dynamic of creation (that it be ruled by humans) was a mistake, nor by declaring that the inner dynamic of his covenant (that Israel would be the means of saving the nations) was a failure, but rather by fulfilling them both. That is more or less what Paul's letter to the Romans is all about.

"This is the purpose that has been realized in Jesus Christ. One of the greatest problems of the Western church, ever since the Reformation at least, is that it hasn't really known what the gospels were there for. Imagining that the point of Christianity was to enable people to go to heaven, most Western Christians supposed that the mechanism by which this happened was the one they found in the writings of Paul (I stress, the one *they found*; I have argued elsewhere that this involved misunderstanding Paul as well) and that the four gospels were simply there to give backup information about Jesus, his teaching, his moral example, and his atoning death. This long tradition screened out the possibility that when Jesus spoke of God's kingdom, he was talking not about a heaven for which he was preparing his followers but about something that was happening in and on this earth, through his work, then through his death and resurrection, and then through the Spirit-led work to which they would be called.

"Part of the difficulty people still have in coming to terms with the gospels, read in this way, is that *kingdom of God* has been a flag of convenience under which all sorts of ships have sailed. Some used the phrase as a cover for pursuing business of their own—programs of moral, social, or political improvement or upheaval, agendas of the left and the right, of the well-meaning but muddled and of the less well-meaning but all too clear. Many who went this route treated the gospels as though they were simply stories about Jesus going around helping people as best he could, with the unfortunate sequel of his untimely death. And many other Christians, seeing this shallow and confused exegesis and application, reacted angrily against what is called kingdom theology as though it were simply an outdated and shallow corporate version of faddish self-help moralism. (This is a serious problem in some parts of America, where *kingdom* has become a slogan of this kind and has then been used to rule out or marginalize many aspects of orthodox Christian faith—precipitating among some would-be orthodox Christians a reaction against any social or political dimension to the gospel and against kingdom language altogether. By such means do we project our own confusions onto the text.)

"But the fact that some people, and some movements, have misappropriated the kingdom theology of the gospels doesn't mean there isn't a reality of which such ideas are a caricature. What we find in the gospels is much, much more profound. Here we meet again a familiar problem, the problem of how Jesus's initial ministry joins up with his self-giving to death. I have argued at length elsewhere that Jesus never imagined that the kingdom he was launching through his healings, feastings, and teachings would be fulfilled without his death. Or, to put it the other way around, I and others have stressed that Jesus's death was not (and he did not think it was) about something other than the kingdom work to which he had devoted his short public career. The problem of evil, which looms up as the backdrop to the gospels, is not going to be dealt with even by Jesus's healings, feastings, and teachings. It certainly won't be dealt with by his then providing his followers with a fast-track route to a distant and disembodied heaven. It can only be dealt with—the kingdom can only come on earth as in heaven—through Jesus's own death and resurrection. That is a whole other story, though of course a central and vital one.

"But when we reintegrate what should never have been separated—the kingdom-inaugurating public work of Jesus and his redemptive death and resurrection—we find that the gospels tell a different story. It isn't just a story of some splendid and exciting social work with an unhappy conclusion. Nor is it just a story of an atoning death with an extended introduction. It is something much bigger than the sum of those two diminished perspectives. It is the story of God's kingdom being launched on earth as in heaven, generating a new state of affairs in which the power of evil has been decisively defeated, the new creation has been decisively launched, and Jesus's followers have been commissioned and equipped to put that victory and that inaugurated new world into practice. Atonement, redemption, and salvation are what happen on the way because engaging in this work demands that people themselves be rescued from the powers that enslave the world in order that they can in turn be rescuers. To put it another way, if you want to help inaugurate God's kingdom, you must follow in the way of the cross, and if you want to benefit from Jesus's saving death, you must become part of his kingdom project. There is only one Jesus, only one gospel story, albeit told in four kaleidoscopic patterns.

"Heaven's rule, God's rule, is thus to be put into practice in the world, resulting in salvation in both the present and the future, a salvation that is both *for* humans and, *through* saved humans, for the wider world. This is the solid basis for the mission of the church. But to explore this further will need another chapter."[12]

Record any insights from the brief commentary and quotes:

Think Through the Issues

This entire study of realizing that Christ's grand strategy is the Church in the context of God building His kingdom should shape every aspect of our understanding of the world and our involvement in it. Nothing can stop the growth of the Church, but it will be opposed by the nations until Christ returns. Only then will the nations understand. This metanarrative—grand strategy—will eventually win over every grand strategy the nations of the world can design. Eventually all the nations will gather against God and His grand strategy.

While Israel no longer exists as the nation who presents God to the world and causes all of the nations to eventually be blessed (it is now the Church in which Jews and Gentiles are one in the churches), God will not forget His promises to the nation of Israel. Jesus will return to fight for Israel when the nations all gather against her. Then, as a nation, Israel will finally understand, and most will believe at that time. In this session, we will examine how we should live in a world as individuals and churches in light of this grand strategy. We will examine how to build it into our proclamation as we share with others Christ's grand strategy for the Church, since the kingdom has now been inaugurated.

ISSUE: Living in the world until Jesus returns

Think Through the Issue Before Discussion:

1. How should the Matthew 23:37–24:31 and the other session 9 passages shape our understanding of world events? How should these passages shape our perspectives and attitudes toward Israel today, because of these events?
2. In what ways can you see the world events aligning themselves with God's plan?
3. In what ways should this part of the Story be part of our proclamation? How does this affect your confidence in the Story?
4. Since the kingdom has been inaugurated and we are at the heart of that kingdom, how should we live in the kingdom until Jesus returns?

Record your initial thoughts on the issue before discussion:

Discuss the issue in your small group.

Record your initial thoughts on the issue after discussion:

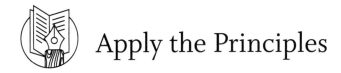# Apply the Principles

It is now time to respond to what you have studied and discussed. Take your time on this section.

Think Back Through the First Three Steps.

Design an Application for Your Life.

Summarize how you see world events aligning with Christ's grand strategy. Record your thoughts on how you might use that as a powerful apologetic in sharing the Story with those in your sphere of influence. Reflect on your own life: How does that build your confidence in the authenticity of God's Story as the true metanarrative in the postmodern world in which we live.

RESHAPING OUR LIVES 🔟

We now have had our minds opened to understanding the Scriptures, just as the two disciples did as they walked along the road to Emmaus just after His resurrection. We know the whole Story. We have walked through the Law, the Prophets, and the Writings with Jesus' disciples through their writings, because that is what they did! They opened the Scriptures to the early churches, just as Jesus did on that road to Emmaus.

It is now time to pull together all of our applications from the first nine sessions, in order to affect our whole lives. In this fast-paced world, it is hard to find time to do any serious reflection. While we have benefited from the exercises in the first nine sessions, actually integrating the truths into our lives as a whole takes extra effort. Taken together, they can become a powerful force bringing about significant change—change designed to reshape our lives.

Committing Your Heart
REFLECTION, PERSONAL JOURNALING, AND PRAYER

Journaling is an excellent way of reflecting more deeply about the significance of what we have been learning. It forces us to express in words what has entered our hearts. It helps us identify and clarify what the Spirit has been using in the Word to enlighten our hearts, as well as to convict us. Prayer should follow this. We should ask God to permanently transform our hearts, to give us a desire and longing to grow to maturity.

In this section, think back over your work from each of the nine previous sessions. What happened in your life because of your work in each session? Record your thoughts, and reflect on what you wrote. What new convictions have you developed? What have you seen God begin to do in your life? Are there areas you wish you had followed through on more fully? What affected you most? What convicted you most? What excited you most? How has your philosophy of Bible study changed?

Finally, formulate these thoughts into one main prayer request. If you were to ask God to make His Story come alive in your life, how would you ask it? Write the request in a paragraph. Transfer it to a 3- x 5-inch card and carry it with you. Pray over it regularly. Over the next few weeks, record on the back of the card, any ways you see God answering your prayer.

Your Journal—thoughts on the importance of the Story to your life and your personal story:

Prayer Request:

Committing Your Mind
FORMING CLEAR CONVICTIONS AND MEMORIZING SCRIPTURE

It is essential that we pull together what we have studied—formulating our thoughts into clear convictions. What is the essence of the Story? What are the core elements you would need to emphasize in order to tell the Story in a short conversation with someone else? What will it take to grasp the whole Story of the Bible? What are the implications of the Story in shaping your own story? The answers to these questions are critical to following Jesus and His grand strategy and to introducing that Story to someone else, thus opening their minds to understanding the Scriptures.

Begin by summarizing the essence of the Story and why you believe it is true—ideally bringing together all of the key truths that you have studied in the nine sessions. Then, list the essential Bible references to back up your convictions. Finally, choose at least one of these verses to memorize, record it below, and quote it by memory to your study group when you meet. Transfer it to a 3- x 5-inch card—writing the verse(s) and reference on one side and your insights into the verse(s) on the other side. Review it for about six weeks.

Summarize the essence of the Story in a few short paragraphs that you could share with someone else.

Key verse to memorize:

Committing Your Life
DECISIONS, PERSONAL PROJECTS, AND LIFE HABITS

Think back over the "Apply the Principles" section of each of the nine sessions. It is one thing to think about specific applications for our lives as we move through each study. It is another thing to think across our whole lives and begin reshaping our life goals and lifestyles by what we are learning. This is a vital part of embracing the Story and allowing it to shape our story. Several things are necessary in order to integrate these principles into our lives. As you look back over your "Apply the Principles" sections and your work so far in this session, ask yourself these questions: Do you need to formally decide the Story is true and clearly make a decision to follow Christ? Do you need to examine your own story in light of the Story and begin shaping your story to align it with the Story? Are there people you need to begin sharing the Story with? Also, what do you need to do over the next few weeks to begin implementing your long-term strategy that you designed in session nine?

Summarize your own story in light of the Story so you can share with others how you embraced the Story and how you would share that the Story points to Christ.

Think through how your own story (your life) needs to be reshaped in light of Christ and His grand strategy.

ENDNOTES

1. Keith Gilmore, an originator of the Bible Walk Thru, taught it in eastern Iowa and all over the Houston, Texas, area since the 1960s. He and Ralph Braun were classmates at Dallas Theological Seminary, class of 1960. Ralph wrote his dissertaion on the Walk-Through and acknowledged Keith's contribution in the preface. I learned the Walk Thru orally from Keith in 1970 in Cedar Rapids, Iowa. I taught over 25 Walk Throughs in the early and mid 70s as we planted the church in Ames, Iowa. Keith went to be with the Lord June 5, 2016.

2. Walter C. Kaiser Jr., The Promise-Plan of God: A Biblical Theology of the Old and New Testaments (Zondervan Kindle Edition, 2009-10-06) Location 276; (Grand Rapids: Zondervan, 2008) pp. 18-19.

3. James D. G. Dunn, Unity and Diversity in the New Testament: An Inquiry into the Character of Earliest Christianity (London: SCM Press, 1977) pp. 81–82.

4. C. H. Dodd, According to the Scriptures: The Sub-structure of New Testament Theology, (London: Fontana Books, 1965) pp. 1–3.

5. Walter C. Kaiser Jr., Recovering the Unity of the Bible: One Continuous Story, Plan, and Purpose (Zondervan Kindle Edition, 2009-10-20), Locations 951–952; (Grand Rapids: Zondervan, 2009) pp. 48-49.

6. Kaiser, Recovering, Kindle Locations 3052–3053; pp. 143-145.

7. Ibid., Kindle Locations 3067–3068; pp. 145-146.

8. Ibid., Kindle Locations 3105–3110; pp. 146-148

9. Ibid., Kindle Locations 3139–3140; pp. 148-150

10. N. T. Wright, Surprised by Hope (HarperCollins. Kindle Edition, 2009-04-24) Locations: 3615-3683 (New York: HarperCollins, 2008), p. 238

11. N. T. Wright, Pauline Perspectives: Essays on Paul, 1978–2013 (Fortress Press Kindle Edition 2013-11-01) Kindle Locations 10430-10477 (Minneapolis: Fortress Press, 2013), pp. 410–411.

12. Wright, Surprised, Kindle Locations 3131-3193; pp. 201–205.

GLOSSARY OF KEY BIBLICAL TERMS AND CONCEPTS

The following is a list of important terms from this study that you may have encountered for the first time. Although they are explained in the booklet, it is easy to forget their exact meanings. This glossary can also serve as a catalogue of biblical terms and concepts for future reference.

EMMAUS ROAD STORY. This refers to Jesus' conversation with two of His disciples on the road to a town near Jerusalem. In that conversation, He opened up the Scriptures to them, unfolding how God fulfilled His plan for mankind through Jesus, who would bring about the kindgom, thus making God's metanarrative of history a reality as He is unfolding it.

METANARRATIVE. A postmodern term that refers to a big story—the story that all other stories fit under. Postmoderns believe that there is no one right story of the world—no metanarrative. Rather, there are many worldviews and many stories, and no one can know the answers to life.

POSTMODERN. A concept referring to the era of history we have entered. It is after the era we call the *modern era*, which was preceded by what we call the *premodern era*. With the emergence of Western science in the modern era, about 500 years old, man believed we could understand everything in the world, create one grand narrative (story of life), and solve all man's problems, destroying the mysticism of the premodern, medieval worldview. But with the crash of this belief, due to the world wars of the 20th century, we entered a postmodern world in which no one believes in one grand story that explains all of life. People are left to their own little stories and are thus without hope.

THE INAUGURATION OF THE KINGDOM. Jesus is the promised king who will sit on the throne of God's coming kingdom. The kingdom was inaugurated at the ascension of Jesus to heaven and the coming of the Spirit in Acts 2. It started out small and is growing worldwide. It will be fully realized at the promised return of Christ.

CHRIST'S GRAND STRATEGY THROUGH THE CHURCH. Many people believe that Christ's grand strategy is embedded in the Gospels, sort of a strategy of individuals discipling other individuals, multiplying, and reaching the world. It is not. Jesus said go wait for the Spirit to come after I leave, and I will tell you My plan in detail. Then He gradually unfolded His strategy for growing the kingdom; it was through the Church. The Church is the center of His plan. He is the head of the Church, and even the rulers and authorities in heaven will be amazed as His plan unfolds. His Church is a worldwide movement with churches that continue to multiply churches until He returns. It is His grand strategy.

BIBLICAL THEOLOGY. *Biblical theology* is a term for a systematic, disciplined study of the Bible, beginning with a grasp of the whole unfolding Story of the Bible, then studying the books of the Bible in the order they were written, beginning with the Old Testament. It involves discovering the author's intent for a book, its literary design, and the theology of each book. As books unfold, they are put into collections like the Law (the Pentateuch—the first five books of Moses). This is called a *canonical section*, thus creating the theology of the Law. As each canonical section is completed in the Old Testament (the Law, the Prophets, and the Writings), then we have what we call an *Old Testament theology*. It's the same in the New Testament. Once both are done, then we have what is called *biblical theology*. It is the only way to validate the meaning of the texts themselves.

OLD TESTAMENT THEOLOGY. A study of the overall plan of the Law, the Prophets, and the Writings—the Jewish Scriptures that we now call the Old Testament. See "Biblical Theology."

NEW TESTAMENT THEOLOGY. *New Testament Theology* is a continued study of the unfolding plan of God, studying the author's intent, literary design, and theology of each book in the order it was written. Most people do not know it, but the first collection written in the New Testament was written by the Apostle Paul. The study of his complete collection is called *Pauline Theology*. The other New Testament collections include Peter's writings, then John's—thus *Petrine Theology* and *Johnannine Theology*. Towards the end of the collections the Gospels were written. When this is all put together it is called *New Testament Theology*.

THE KERYGMA. *The kerygma* is the Greek term which means "the proclamation." It is used to explain the gospel story. This is the essence of the kerygma: Jesus was prophesied about in the Old Testament; lived life on earth as a man, doing good and healing; died, was buried, resurrected, and ascended to heaven; and will return as king and judge. Everyone who believes in Him will have forgiveness of sins. The Early Church called this *the kerygma*.

THE DIDACHE. This is the Greek word for "the teaching." It refers to the teaching Jesus Christ delivered to the Apostles, especially to Paul, as He promised through the Spirit. This teaching is also called *the faith*, *the deposit*, *the sound doctrine*. The early churches called this body of teaching *the didache*.

THE COVENANTS AND GOD'S UNFOLDING PLAN. Several covenants were made as the Story unfolded: The Abrahamic Covenant, the Law Covenant, the Davidic Covenant, and the New Covenant. But since one builds upon another in the context of one unfolding Story and plan, they together make up one big covenant by God to bless all the families of the earth.

THE MYSTERY (SURPRISE) OF THE CHURCH. The Church was God's big surprise. The word *mystery* means something not previously revealed. After Christ left, His Jewish followers thought the new community was going to be within Israel, but the surprise was that Christ developed a new grand strategy for building His kingdom. That new strategy was the Church, in the form of a worldwide multiplication of churches who would drive the progress of the gospel. The Church was a hidden part of the Story of the unfolding plan of God to build His kingdom.

LIFELONG LEARNING

We recommend the following resources to help you more fully understand the Story and more fully align your own story with God's Story, specifically Christ's grand strategy. The First Principles Series will help you shape your life, family, and work around Christ's grand strategy, the Church. Series 1 and 2 of the Mastering the Scriptures Series will build carefully on the foundation of *The Story* and The First Principles, thus strengthening your own faith and effectiveness in ministry and laying a lifetime foundation for mastering the Scriptures. I included Kaiser's collection because it is critical that good Old Testament theology foundations are laid; he is the father of Old Testament theology.

1. The First Principles Series

This is a collection of 13 booklets, divided into three series, designed to be a serious ordered learning system, which normally takes three years to complete. In one sense, it is a modern catechism, built around *the didache*. It is fully integrated with *The Story*, both building on it and following the same educational style.

2. Mastering the Scriptures Series

This is a collection of Old and New Testament booklets designed to build on the foundation of *The Story* and *The First Principles Series*. The first two series of the New Testament Collections will be released in 2016 and 2018.

> Series 1: The Gospels (5 booklets, released late fall 2016 to early 2017)
>
>> This is a series of five booklets on the four Gospels, designed to follow up The First Principles Series. It develops out the kerygma just as The First Principles Series did the didache. The Gospels were designed to fully stabilize networks of churches in the kerygma.
>
> Series 2: Paul's Early Letters (6 booklets, to be released late fall 2017 and early 2018)
>
>> This is a series of booklets designed to build on The Gospels, in which Paul fully develops the kerygma and its implications for his churches, to fully establish the churches in the gospel. Paul's early letters include: Galatians, 1 and 2 Thessalonians, 1 and 2 Corinthians, and Romans.

3. Walter C. Kaiser Collections

Kaiser is considered the father of Old Testament Theology. He has been my personal mentor since 1974. I have divided his works into 2 collections, which are the heart of his massive work of books and journal articles. The first collection is for every believer and for modal leaders; the second is for more scholarly believers and sodal leaders.

Collection 1: BILD Institute Level
- A. *Recovering the Unity of the Bible: One Continuous Story, Plan, and Purpose*
- B. *The Promise-Plan of God: A Biblical Theology of the Old and New Testaments*

Collection 2: Antioch School Level
- A. *Toward an Old Testament Theology*
- B. *Toward an Exegetical Theology*
- C. *Toward an Old Testament Ethic*
- D. *Toward the Use of the Old Testament in the New*

APPENDIX A: THE UNFOLDING GRAND STRATEGY

The Grand Strategy Unfolds (metanarrative): Genesis 12:1–3, The Abrahamic Covenant, the Promise

1. God chose one man and his family to build a nation that would eventually bless all the nations of the world.
2. He specifically made a covenant with that man, Abraham, to bring about the fulfillment of the promise, which would solve the problem of the nations continually rejecting God (Genesis 1–11).
3. This nation would be based in the land of Canaan (from the river of Egypt to the Euphrates) and would grow from Abraham's own ancestral line—through Isaac.
4. Abraham's own righteousness was based on faith in this promise, not on some personal righteousness attained by his own efforts.

The Grand Strategy Unfolds (metanarrative): Exodus 19:1–6, The Mosaic Covenant, The Law (embedded in the Promise).

1. God made a covenant with Israel, the nation promised to Abraham, to bless all the families of the earth.
2. His intention was for that nation to be a nation that introduced God to the nations—"a priestly kingdom and a holy nation."
3. At the foundation of the nation was a set of "first principles" (The Ten Commandments), designed to make them holy.
4. They would not be able to obey the covenant until a future time when God would change their hearts permanently.
5. In the future, a prophet would come in the tradition of Moses, through whom God would explain everything. Peter saw this prophet as Jesus.

The Grand Strategy Unfolds (metanarrative): 2 Samuel 7:1–29, The Davidic Covenant

1. God made a covenant with David that his kingdom and his throne would last forever.
2. The future king would come from Galilee and would be both God and man.
3. David foresaw this king as his Lord and that He would not undergo decay but would sit at the right hand of God (predicting the resurrection).

4. David saw this as part of the plan of God, of making Israel a great nation and of making a great name for Himself, and David used the Psalms to build this instruction into the people of God.

The Grand Strategy Unfolds (metanarrative): Mark 1:1–15, The Kingdom Arrives, The Plan for the History of Mankind (developed further)

1. Jesus arrived on the scene, proclaiming the good news (the kerygma): the kingdom of God is at hand.
2. Jesus identified Himself as the Son of God, the coming king promised in the prophecies of the Old Testament.
3. The essence of that good news was revealed: He would be killed, buried, and resurrected, and those who believe in Him would be part of His kingdom.
4. Those who believed, a small group of followers who remained with Him after His resurrection and ascension, were to proclaim this good news, this gospel, to the whole world. (Remember Genesis 12:1–3.)
5. Peter proclaimed this gospel in early Acts in 5 sermons.
6. Paul stated this gospel—the good news—in formula form and affirmed having received it from the Apostles.

The Grand Strategy Unfolds (metanarrative): Acts 1:1–8, The Kingdom Launched

1. Jesus told His disciples that they were to be witnesses in Jerusalem, Judea and Samaria, and to all nations.
2. Jesus told the disciples to go and wait for instructions from the Spirit on how to carry out their witness.
3. They proclaimed the gospel and gathered believers into new communities formed around the Apostles' teaching.
4. The witness to the nations was given shape through specific work given to Paul and his team.
5. They proclaimed the gospel in and around strategic cities.
6. They instructed the new believers—the Apostles' teaching.
7. They formed the believers into churches and appointed elders in every church.

The Grand Strategy Unfolds (metanarrative): Ephesians 2:11–4:26, The Church—Christ's Grand Strategy

1. Christ's plan—the Church—was a mystery, something not previously revealed (Eph. 3:3 "the mystery was made known to me by revelation").

2. Paul's stewardship was (1) to preach the gospel to the Gentiles and (2) "to bring to light the plan of the mystery"—the mystery being Christ and His plan, previously hidden.
3. Paul also revealed Christ's specific strategy for the community life of His churches. A church is a family of families, which by its community life will show the beauty of Christ.
4. As a result, Jews and Gentiles are now one in Christ in the Church, which was God's previously hidden plan.
5. The Church has one foundation: the one laid by the Apostles and prophets, with Jesus as the cornerstone.
6. There is only one foundation: one body, one Spirit, one hope of your calling, one Lord, one faith (one body of teaching), one baptism, one God and Father.
7. Apostles, prophets, evangelists, and pastors and teachers are to build up the Church on that one foundation. Then, when each one is doing his or her part, in harmony, people can see Christ in His fullness.
8. Even the rulers and authorities in the heavenly places would be amazed at the wisdom of God through the Church.
9. Jesus predicted He would build His church, and nothing of Satan and this world could stop it.
10. Though it was Paul's job to fully bring to light Christ's plan through His Church, Peter rooted its foundation in the prophecies of the Old Testament: Jesus is the cornerstone of this new global people, the Church.

The Grand Strategy Unfolds (metanarrative): Matthew 24:1–31, The Kingdom Fully Realized

1. Israel's house (as promised through the line of David) will be left desolate until Christ returns, since He is the promised king from the line of David. Israel will undergo an era of being hated by all nations, filled with many false messiahs.
2. Before the end comes and the kingdom is fully realized, there will be a great increase of wars (nation against nation) and an increase of natural catastrophes. A final hatred of Israel will culminate, led by a world leader (predicted by Daniel) who would destroy Israel were it not for the return of Christ. The Church, God's new people, will be persecuted and hated by the nations as well.
3. In the day of Christ's return, He will gather all nations to a battle against Israel. Christ will then return and defeat the nations in a great battle and fully establish His kingdom. Jerusalem will be the center of this kingdom. Christ will be king over all the earth, and everyone will know who He is.

4. Not all Israelites belong to Israel. Though they are heirs of all the promises, only those who have faith in God through the promises belong to Israel (saved by faith not flesh). Israel has zeal but has not been enlightened.

5. A partial hardening has come over the nations until all the Gentiles are brought into the kingdom; then Israel as a whole will respond. Therefore, we as Gentiles should not be arrogant, but we should enlighten ourselves as to God's enduring promises to Israel. Whereas just a few from the nation of Israel believed at the inauguration of the kingdom in early Acts, the nation as a whole (not everyone) will respond and believe at the return of Christ.

6. The return will not be until the good news of the kingdom (the gospel, the kerygma) is proclaimed to the whole world. When Christ returns, He will gather His people—His kingdom—from all peoples of the world and fully inaugurate His kingdom. Our job is to proclaim the gospel to the whole world until the return of Christ.

APPENDIX B: THE STORY: TESTIMONIES

OLD TESTAMENT

Genesis 12:1–3
Now the LORD said to Abram, "Go from your country and your kindred and your father's house to the land that I will show you. 2 I will make of you a great nation, and I will bless you, and make your name great, so that you will be a blessing. 3 I will bless those who bless you, and the one who curses you I will curse; and in you all the families of the earth shall be blessed."

Genesis 15:1–6
After these things the word of the LORD came to Abram in a vision, "Do not be afraid, Abram, I am your shield; your reward shall be very great." 2 But Abram said, "O Lord GOD, what will you give me, for I continue childless, and the heir of my house is Eliezer of Damascus?" 3 And Abram said, "You have given me no offspring, and so a slave born in my house is to be my heir." 4 But the word of the LORD came to him, "This man shall not be your heir; no one but your very own issue shall be your heir." 5 He brought him outside and said, "Look toward heaven and count the stars, if you are able to count them." Then he said to him, "So shall your descendants be." 6 And he believed the LORD; and the LORD reckoned it to him as righteousness.

Genesis 17:1–8
When Abram was ninety-nine years old, the LORD appeared to Abram, and said to him, "I am God Almighty; walk before me, and be blameless. 2 And I will make my covenant between me and you, and will make you exceedingly numerous." 3 Then Abram fell on his face; and God said to him, 4 "As for me, this is my covenant with you: You shall be the ancestor of a multitude of nations. 5 No longer shall your name be Abram, but your name shall be Abraham, for I have made you the ancestor of a multitude of nations. 6 I will make you exceedingly fruitful; and I will make nations of you, and kings shall come from you. 7 I will establish my covenant between me and you, and your offspring after you throughout their generations, for an everlasting covenant, to be God to you and to your offspring after you. 8 And I will give to you and to your offspring after you, the land where you are now an alien, all the land of Canaan, for a perpetual holding; and I will be their God."

Exodus 19:1–6
On the third new moon after the Israelites had gone out of the land of Egypt, on that very day, they came into the wilderness of Sinai. 2 They had journeyed from Rephidim, entered the wilderness of Sinai, and camped in the wilderness; Israel camped there in

front of the mountain. 3 Then Moses went up to God; the LORD called to him from the mountain, saying, "Thus you shall say to the house of Jacob, and tell the Israelites: 4 You have seen what I did to the Egyptians, and how I bore you on eagles' wings and brought you to myself. 5 Now therefore, if you obey my voice and keep my covenant, you shall be my treasured possession out of all the peoples. Indeed, the whole earth is mine, 6 but you shall be for me a priestly kingdom and a holy nation. These are the words that you shall speak to the Israelites."

Exodus 20: 1–17
Then God spoke all these words:

2 I am the LORD your God, who brought you out of the land of Egypt, out of the house of slavery; 3 you shall have no other gods before me.

4 You shall not make for yourself an idol, whether in the form of anything that is in heaven above, or that is on the earth beneath, or that is in the water under the earth. 5 You shall not bow down to them or worship them; for I the LORD your God am a jealous God, punishing children for the iniquity of parents, to the third and the fourth generation of those who reject me, 6 but showing steadfast love to the thousandth generation of those who love me and keep my commandments.

7 You shall not make wrongful use of the name of the LORD your God, for the LORD will not acquit anyone who misuses his name.

8 Remember the Sabbath day, and keep it holy. 9 Six days you shall labor and do all your work. 10 But the seventh day is a Sabbath to the LORD your God; you shall not do any work—you, your son or your daughter, your male or female slave, your livestock, or the alien resident in your towns. 11 For in six days the LORD made heaven and earth, the sea, and all that is in them, but rested the seventh day; therefore the LORD blessed the Sabbath day and consecrated it.

12 Honor your father and your mother, so that your days may be long in the land that the LORD your God is giving you.

13 You shall not murder.

14 You shall not commit adultery.

15 You shall not steal.

16 You shall not bear false witness against your neighbor.

17 You shall not covet your neighbor's house; you shall not covet your neighbor's wife, or male or female slave, or ox, or donkey, or anything that belongs to your neighbor.

Deuteronomy 18:15–19

15 The LORD your God will raise up for you a prophet like me from among your own people; you shall heed such a prophet. 16 This is what you requested of the LORD your God at Horeb on the day of the assembly when you said: "If I hear the voice of the LORD my God any more, or ever again see this great fire, I will die." 17 Then the LORD replied to me: "They are right in what they have said. 18 I will raise up for them a prophet like you from among their own people; I will put my words in the mouth of the prophet, who shall speak to them everything that I command. 19 Anyone who does not heed the words that the prophet shall speak in my name, I myself will hold accountable.

Deuteronomy 30:1–10

When all these things have happened to you, the blessings and the curses that I have set before you, if you call them to mind among all the nations where the LORD your God has driven you, 2 and return to the LORD your God, and you and your children obey him with all your heart and with all your soul, just as I am commanding you today, 3 then the LORD your God will restore your fortunes and have compassion on you, gathering you again from all the peoples among whom the LORD your God has scattered you. 4 Even if you are exiled to the ends of the world, from there the LORD your God will gather you, and from there he will bring you back. 5 The LORD your God will bring you into the land that your ancestors possessed, and you will possess it; he will make you more prosperous and numerous than your ancestors.

6 Moreover, the LORD your God will circumcise your heart and the heart of your descendants, so that you will love the LORD your God with all your heart and with all your soul, in order that you may live. 7 The LORD your God will put all these curses on your enemies and on the adversaries who took advantage of you. 8 Then you shall again obey the LORD, observing all his commandments that I am commanding you today, 9 and the LORD your God will make you abundantly prosperous in all your undertakings, in the fruit of your body, in the fruit of your livestock, and in the fruit of your soil. For the LORD will again take delight in prospering you, just as he delighted in prospering your ancestors, 10 when you obey the LORD your God by observing his commandments and decrees that are written in this book of the law, because you turn to the LORD your God with all your heart and with all your soul.

2 Samuel 7:1–29

7 Now when the king was settled in his house and the LORD had given him rest from all his enemies around him, 2 the king said to the prophet Nathan, "See now, I am living in a house of cedar, but the ark of God stays in a tent." 3 Nathan said to the king, "Go, do all that you have in mind; for the LORD is with you."

4 But that same night the word of the LORD came to Nathan: 5 Go and tell my servant David: Thus says the LORD: Are you the one to build me a house to live in? 6 I have not lived in a house since the day I brought up the people of Israel from Egypt to this day, but I have been moving about in a tent and a tabernacle. 7 Wherever I have moved

about among all the people of Israel, did I ever speak a word with any of the tribal leaders of Israel, whom I commanded to shepherd my people Israel, saying, "Why have you not built me a house of cedar?" 8 Now therefore thus you shall say to my servant David: Thus says the LORD of hosts: I took you from the pasture, from following the sheep to be prince over my people Israel; 9 and I have been with you wherever you went, and have cut off all your enemies from before you; and I will make for you a great name, like the name of the great ones of the earth. 10 And I will appoint a place for my people Israel and will plant them, so that they may live in their own place, and be disturbed no more; and evildoers shall afflict them no more, as formerly, 11 from the time that I appointed judges over my people Israel; and I will give you rest from all your enemies. Moreover the LORD declares to you that the LORD will make you a house. 12 When your days are fulfilled and you lie down with your ancestors, I will raise up your offspring after you, who shall come forth from your body, and I will establish his kingdom. 13 He shall build a house for my name, and I will establish the throne of his kingdom forever. 14 I will be a father to him, and he shall be a son to me. When he commits iniquity, I will punish him with a rod such as mortals use, with blows inflicted by human beings. 15 But I will not take my steadfast love from him, as I took it from Saul, whom I put away from before you. 16 Your house and your kingdom shall be made sure forever before me; your throne shall be established forever. 17 In accordance with all these words and with all this vision, Nathan spoke to David.

18 Then King David went in and sat before the LORD, and said, "Who am I, O Lord GOD, and what is my house, that you have brought me thus far? 19 And yet this was a small thing in your eyes, O Lord GOD; you have spoken also of your servant's house for a great while to come. May this be instruction for the people, O Lord GOD! 20 And what more can David say to you? For you know your servant, O Lord GOD! 21 Because of your promise, and according to your own heart, you have wrought all this greatness, so that your servant may know it. 22 Therefore you are great, O LORD God; for there is no one like you, and there is no God besides you, according to all that we have heard with our ears. 23 Who is like your people, like Israel? Is there another nation on earth whose God went to redeem it as a people, and to make a name for himself, doing great and awesome things for them, by driving out before his people nations and their gods? 24 And you established your people Israel for yourself to be your people forever; and you, O LORD, became their God. 25 And now, O LORD God, as for the word that you have spoken concerning your servant and concerning his house, confirm it forever; do as you have promised. 26 Thus your name will be magnified forever in the saying, 'The LORD of hosts is God over Israel'; and the house of your servant David will be established before you. 27 For you, O LORD of hosts, the God of Israel, have made this revelation to your servant, saying, 'I will build you a house'; therefore your servant has found courage to pray this prayer to you. 28 And now, O Lord GOD, you are God, and your words are true, and you have promised this good thing to your servant; 29 now therefore may it please you to bless the house of your servant, so that it may continue forever before you; for you, O Lord GOD, have spoken, and with your blessing shall the house of your servant be blessed forever."

Psalm 16:8–11

8 I keep the LORD always before me;
   because he is at my right hand, I shall not be moved.
9 Therefore my heart is glad, and my soul rejoices;
   my body also rests secure.
10 For you do not give me up to Sheol,
   or let your faithful one see the Pit.
11 You show me the path of life.
   In your presence there is fullness of joy;
   in your right hand are pleasures forevermore.

Psalm 16:8–11

8 I keep the LORD always before me;
   because he is at my right hand, I shall not be moved.
9 Therefore my heart is glad, and my soul rejoices;
   my body also rests secure.
10 For you do not give me up to Sheol,
   or let your faithful one see the Pit.
11 You show me the path of life.
   In your presence there is fullness of joy;
   in your right hand are pleasures forevermore.

Psalm 89:1–4

1 I will sing of your steadfast love, O LORD, forever;
   with my mouth I will proclaim your faithfulness to all generations.
2 I declare that your steadfast love is established forever;
   your faithfulness is as firm as the heavens.
3 You said, "I have made a covenant with my chosen one,
   I have sworn to my servant David:
4 'I will establish your descendants forever,
   and build your throne for all generations.'"

Psalm 89:30–37

30 If his children forsake my law
   and do not walk according to my ordinances,
31 if they violate my statutes
   and do not keep my commandments,
32 then I will punish their transgression with the rod
   and their iniquity with scourges;
33 but I will not remove from him my steadfast love,
   or be false to my faithfulness.

34 I will not violate my covenant,
   or alter the word that went forth from my lips.
35 Once and for all I have sworn by my holiness;
   I will not lie to David.
36 His line shall continue forever,
   and his throne endure before me like the sun.
37 It shall be established forever like the moon,
   an enduring witness in the skies."

Psalm 110:1–6
1 The LORD says to my lord,
   "Sit at my right hand
until I make your enemies your footstool."
2 The LORD sends out from Zion
   your mighty scepter.
   Rule in the midst of your foes.
3 Your people will offer themselves willingly
   on the day you lead your forces
   on the holy mountains.
From the womb of the morning,
   like dew, your youth will come to you.
4 The LORD has sworn and will not change his mind,
   "You are a priest forever according to the order of Melchizedek."
5 The Lord is at your right hand;
   he will shatter kings on the day of his wrath.
6 He will execute judgment among the nations,
   filling them with corpses;
he will shatter heads
   over the wide earth.

Psalm 118:22–23
22 The stone that the builders rejected
   has become the chief cornerstone.
23 This is the LORD's doing;
   it is marvelous in our eyes.

Isaiah 9:1–7
But there will be no gloom for those who were in anguish. In the former time he brought into contempt the land of Zebulun and the land of Naphtali, but in the latter time he will make glorious the way of the sea, the land beyond the Jordan, Galilee of the nations.

2 The people who walked in darkness
   have seen a great light;
those who lived in a land of deep darkness—
   on them light has shined.
3 You have multiplied the nation,
   you have increased its joy;
they rejoice before you
   as with joy at the harvest,
   as people exult when dividing plunder.
4 For the yoke of their burden,
   and the bar across their shoulders,
   the rod of their oppressor,
   you have broken as on the day of Midian.
5 For all the boots of the tramping warriors
   and all the garments rolled in blood
   shall be burned as fuel for the fire.
6 For a child has been born for us,
   a son given to us;
authority rests upon his shoulders;
   and he is named
Wonderful Counselor, Mighty God,
   Everlasting Father, Prince of Peace.
7 His authority shall grow continually,
   and there shall be endless peace
for the throne of David and his kingdom.
   He will establish and uphold it
with justice and with righteousness
   from this time onward and forevermore.
The zeal of the LORD of hosts will do this.

Isaiah 28:16

16 therefore thus says the Lord GOD,
See, I am laying in Zion a foundation stone,
   a tested stone,
a precious cornerstone, a sure foundation:
   "One who trusts will not panic."

Isaiah 53:1–12

Who has believed what we have heard?
   And to whom has the arm of the LORD been revealed?
2 For he grew up before him like a young plant,
   and like a root out of dry ground;
he had no form or majesty that we should look at him,

nothing in his appearance that we should desire him.
3 He was despised and rejected by others;
   a man of suffering and acquainted with infirmity;
and as one from whom others hide their faces
   he was despised, and we held him of no account.

4 Surely he has borne our infirmities
   and carried our diseases;
yet we accounted him stricken,
   struck down by God, and afflicted.
5 But he was wounded for our transgressions,
   crushed for our iniquities;
upon him was the punishment that made us whole,
   and by his bruises we are healed.
6 All we like sheep have gone astray;
   we have all turned to our own way,
and the LORD has laid on him
   the iniquity of us all.

7 He was oppressed, and he was afflicted,
   yet he did not open his mouth;
like a lamb that is led to the slaughter,
   and like a sheep that before its shearers is silent,
   so he did not open his mouth.
8 By a perversion of justice he was taken away.
   Who could have imagined his future?
For he was cut off from the land of the living,
   stricken for the transgression of my people.
9 They made his grave with the wicked
   and his tomb with the rich,
although he had done no violence,
   and there was no deceit in his mouth.

10 Yet it was the will of the LORD to crush him with pain.
When you make his life an offering for sin,
   he shall see his offspring, and shall prolong his days;
through him the will of the LORD shall prosper.
11   Out of his anguish he shall see light;
he shall find satisfaction through his knowledge.
   The righteous one, my servant, shall make many righteous,
   and he shall bear their iniquities.
12 Therefore I will allot him a portion with the great,
   and he shall divide the spoil with the strong;

because he poured out himself to death,
 and was numbered with the transgressors;
yet he bore the sin of many,
 and made intercession for the transgressors.

Zechariah 14:1–9

14 See, a day is coming for the LORD, when the plunder taken from you will be divided in your midst. 2 For I will gather all the nations against Jerusalem to battle, and the city shall be taken and the houses looted and the women raped; half the city shall go into exile, but the rest of the people shall not be cut off from the city. 3 Then the LORD will go forth and fight against those nations as when he fights on a day of battle. 4 On that day his feet shall stand on the Mount of Olives, which lies before Jerusalem on the east; and the Mount of Olives shall be split in two from east to west by a very wide valley; so that one half of the Mount shall withdraw northward, and the other half southward. 5 And you shall flee by the valley of the LORD's mountain, for the valley between the mountains shall reach to Azal; and you shall flee as you fled from the earthquake in the days of King Uzziah of Judah. Then the LORD my God will come and all the holy ones with him.

6 On that day there shall not be either cold or frost. 7 And there shall be continuous day (it is known to the LORD), not day and not night, for an evening time there shall be light.

8 On that day living waters shall flow out from Jerusalem, half of them to the eastern sea and half of them to the western sea; it shall continue in summer as in winter.

9 And the LORD will become king over all the earth; on that day the LORD will be one and his name one.

NEW TESTAMENT

Matthew 16:13–20

13 Now when Jesus came into the district of Caesarea Philippi, he asked his disciples, "Who do people say that the Son of Man is?" 14 And they said, "Some say John the Baptist, but others Elijah, and still others Jeremiah or one of the prophets." 15 He said to them, "But who do you say that I am?" 16 Simon Peter answered, "You are the Messiah, the Son of the living God." 17 And Jesus answered him, "Blessed are you, Simon son of Jonah! For flesh and blood has not revealed this to you, but my Father in heaven. 18 And I tell you, you are Peter, and on this rock I will build my church, and the gates of Hades will not prevail against it. 19 I will give you the keys of the kingdom of heaven, and whatever you bind on earth will be bound in heaven, and whatever you loose on earth will be loosed in heaven." 20 Then he sternly ordered the disciples not to tell anyone that he was the Messiah.

Matthew 23:37–24:31

37 "Jerusalem, Jerusalem, the city that kills the prophets and stones those who are sent to it! How often have I desired to gather your children together as a hen gathers her brood under her wings, and you were not willing! 38 See, your house is left to you, desolate. 39 For I tell you, you will not see me again until you say, 'Blessed is the one who comes in the name of the Lord.'"

24 As Jesus came out of the temple and was going away, his disciples came to point out to him the buildings of the temple. 2 Then he asked them, "You see all these, do you not? Truly I tell you, not one stone will be left here upon another; all will be thrown down."

3 When he was sitting on the Mount of Olives, the disciples came to him privately, saying, "Tell us, when will this be, and what will be the sign of your coming and of the end of the age?" 4 Jesus answered them, "Beware that no one leads you astray. 5 For many will come in my name, saying, 'I am the Messiah! 'and they will lead many astray. 6 And you will hear of wars and rumors of wars; see that you are not alarmed; for this must take place, but the end is not yet. 7 For nation will rise against nation, and kingdom against kingdom, and there will be famines and earthquakes in various places: 8 all this is but the beginning of the birth pangs.

9 "Then they will hand you over to be tortured and will put you to death, and you will be hated by all nations because of my name. 10 Then many will fall away, and they will betray one another and hate one another. 11 And many false prophets will arise and lead many astray. 12 And because of the increase of lawlessness, the love of many will grow cold. 13 But the one who endures to the end will be saved. 14 And this good news of the kingdom will be proclaimed throughout the world, as a testimony to all the nations; and then the end will come.

15 "So when you see the desolating sacrilege standing in the holy place, as was spoken of by the prophet Daniel (let the reader understand), 16 then those in Judea must flee to the mountains; 17 the one on the housetop must not go down to take what is in the house; 18 the one in the field must not turn back to get a coat. 19 Woe to those who are pregnant and to those who are nursing infants in those days! 20 Pray that your flight may not be in winter or on a Sabbath. 21 For at that time there will be great suffering, such as has not been from the beginning of the world until now, no, and never will be. 22 And if those days had not been cut short, no one would be saved; but for the sake of the elect those days will be cut short. 23 Then if anyone says to you, 'Look! Here is the Messiah!'or 'There he is!'—do not believe it. 24 For false messiahs and false prophets will appear and produce great signs and omens, to lead astray, if possible, even the elect. 25 Take note, I have told you beforehand. 26 So, if they say to you, 'Look! He is in the wilderness,' do not go out. If they say, 'Look! He is in the inner rooms,' do not believe it. 27 For as the lightning comes from the east and flashes as far as the west, so will be the coming of the Son of Man. 28 Wherever the corpse is, there the vultures will gather.

29 "Immediately after the suffering of those days
the sun will be darkened,
    and the moon will not give its light;
the stars will fall from heaven,
    and the powers of heaven will be shaken.
30 Then the sign of the Son of Man will appear in heaven, and then all the tribes of the earth will mourn, and they will see 'the Son of Man coming on the clouds of heaven' with power and great glory. 31 And he will send out his angels with a loud trumpet call, and they will gather his elect from the four winds, from one end of heaven to the other.

Mark 1:1–15

1 The beginning of the good news of Jesus Christ, the Son of God.

2 As it is written in the prophet Isaiah,
"See, I am sending my messenger ahead of you,
    who will prepare your way;
3 the voice of one crying out in the wilderness:
    'Prepare the way of the Lord,
    make his paths straight,'"
4 John the baptizer appeared in the wilderness, proclaiming a baptism of repentance for the forgiveness of sins. 5 And people from the whole Judean countryside and all the people of Jerusalem were going out to him, and were baptized by him in the river Jordan, confessing their sins. 6 Now John was clothed with camel's hair, with a leather belt around his waist, and he ate locusts and wild honey. 7 He proclaimed, "The one who is more powerful than I is coming after me; I am not worthy to stoop down and untie the thong of his sandals. 8 I have baptized you with water; but he will baptize you with the Holy Spirit."

9 In those days Jesus came from Nazareth of Galilee and was baptized by John in the Jordan. 10 And just as he was coming up out of the water, he saw the heavens torn apart and the Spirit descending like a dove on him. 11 And a voice came from heaven, "You are my Son, the Beloved; with you I am well pleased."

12 And the Spirit immediately drove him out into the wilderness. 13 He was in the wilderness forty days, tempted by Satan; and he was with the wild beasts; and the angels waited on him.

The Beginning of the Galilean Ministry

14 Now after John was arrested, Jesus came to Galilee, proclaiming the good news of God, 15 and saying, "The time is fulfilled, and the kingdom of God has come near; repent, and believe in the good news."

Mark 8:27–31

Jesus went on with his disciples to the villages of Caesarea Philippi; and on the way he asked his disciples, "Who do people say that I am?" 28 And they answered him, "John the Baptist; and others, Elijah; and still others, one of the prophets." 29 He asked them, "But who do you say that I am?" Peter answered him, "You are the Messiah." 30 And he sternly ordered them not to tell anyone about him. 31 Then he began to teach them that the Son of Man must undergo great suffering, and be rejected by the elders, the chief priests, and the scribes, and be killed, and after three days rise again.

Mark 9:30–32

30 They went on from there and passed through Galilee. He did not want anyone to know it; 31 for he was teaching his disciples, saying to them, "The Son of Man is to be betrayed into human hands, and they will kill him, and three days after being killed, he will rise again." 32 But they did not understand what he was saying and were afraid to ask him.

Mark 10:32–34

32 They were on the road, going up to Jerusalem, and Jesus was walking ahead of them; they were amazed, and those who followed were afraid. He took the twelve aside again and began to tell them what was to happen to him, 33 saying, "See, we are going up to Jerusalem, and the Son of Man will be handed over to the chief priests and the scribes, and they will condemn him to death; then they will hand him over to the Gentiles; 34 they will mock him, and spit upon him, and flog him, and kill him; and after three days he will rise again."

Mark 12:35–37

35 While Jesus was teaching in the temple, he said, "How can the scribes say that the Messiah[a] is the son of David? 36 David himself, by the Holy Spirit, declared,

'The Lord said to my Lord,
"Sit at my right hand,
   until I put your enemies under your feet."'

37 David himself calls him Lord; so how can he be his son?" And the large crowd was listening to him with delight.

Mark 14:22–25

22 While they were eating, he took a loaf of bread, and after blessing it he broke it, gave it to them, and said, "Take; this is my body." 23 Then he took a cup, and after giving thanks he gave it to them, and all of them drank from it. 24 He said to them, "This is my blood of the covenant, which is poured out for many. 25 Truly I tell you, I will never again drink of the fruit of the vine until that day when I drink it new in the kingdom of God."

Mark 16:14-18

14 Later he appeared to the eleven themselves as they were sitting at the table; and he upbraided them for their lack of faith and stubbornness, because they had not believed those who saw him after he had risen. 15 And he said to them, "Go into all the world and proclaim the good news to the whole creation. 16 The one who believes and is baptized will be saved; but the one who does not believe will be condemned. 17 And these signs will accompany those who believe: by using my name they will cast out demons; they will speak in new tongues; 18 they will pick up snakes in their hands, and if they drink any deadly thing, it will not hurt them; they will lay their hands on the sick, and they will recover."

Luke 24:13-27

13 Now on that same day two of them were going to a village called Emmaus, about seven miles from Jerusalem, 14 and talking with each other about all these things that had happened. 15 While they were talking and discussing, Jesus himself came near and went with them, 16 but their eyes were kept from recognizing him. 17 And he said to them, "What are you discussing with each other while you walk along?" They stood still, looking sad. 18 Then one of them, whose name was Cleopas, answered him, "Are you the only stranger in Jerusalem who does not know the things that have taken place there in these days?" 19 He asked them, "What things?" They replied, "The things about Jesus of Nazareth, who was a prophet mighty in deed and word before God and all the people, 20 and how our chief priests and leaders handed him over to be condemned to death and crucified him. 21 But we had hoped that he was the one to redeem Israel. Yes, and besides all this, it is now the third day since these things took place. 22 Moreover, some women of our group astounded us. They were at the tomb early this morning, 23 and when they did not find his body there; they came back and told us that they had indeed seen a vision of angels who said that he was alive. 24 Some of those who were with us went to the tomb and found it just as the women had said; but they did not see him." 25 Then he said to them, "Oh, how foolish you are, and how slow of heart to believe all that the prophets have declared! 26 Was it not necessary that the Messiah should suffer these things and then enter into his glory?" 27 Then beginning with Moses and all the prophets, he interpreted to them the things about himself in all the scriptures.

Luke 24:44-49

44 Then he said to them, "These are my words that I spoke to you while I was still with you—that everything written about me in the law of Moses, the prophets, and the psalms must be fulfilled." 45 Then he opened their minds to understand the scriptures, 46 and he said to them, "Thus it is written, that the Messiah is to suffer and to rise from the dead on the third day, 47 and that repentance and forgiveness of sins is to be proclaimed in his name to all nations, beginning from Jerusalem. 48 You are witnesses of these things. 49 And see, I am sending upon you what my Father promised; so stay here in the city until you have been clothed with power from on high."

Acts 1:1–11

1 In the first book, Theophilus, I wrote about all that Jesus did and taught from the beginning 2 until the day when he was taken up to heaven, after giving instructions through the Holy Spirit to the apostles whom he had chosen. 3 After his suffering he presented himself alive to them by many convincing proofs, appearing to them during forty days and speaking about the kingdom of God. 4 While staying with them, he ordered them not to leave Jerusalem, but to wait there for the promise of the Father. "This," he said, "is what you have heard from me; 5 for John baptized with water, but you will be baptized with the Holy Spirit not many days from now."

6 So when they had come together, they asked him, "Lord, is this the time when you will restore the kingdom to Israel?" 7 He replied, "It is not for you to know the times or periods that the Father has set by his own authority. 8 But you will receive power when the Holy Spirit has come upon you; and you will be my witnesses in Jerusalem, in all Judea and Samaria, and to the ends of the earth." 9 When he had said this, as they were watching, he was lifted up, and a cloud took him out of their sight. 10 While he was going and they were gazing up toward heaven, suddenly two men in white robes stood by them. 11 They said, "Men of Galilee, why do you stand looking up toward heaven? This Jesus, who has been taken up from you into heaven, will come in the same way as you saw him go into heaven."

Acts 2:42–47

42 They devoted themselves to the apostles' teaching and fellowship, to the breaking of bread and the prayers.

43 Awe came upon everyone, because many wonders and signs were being done by the apostles. 44 All who believed were together and had all things in common; 45 they would sell their possessions and goods and distribute the proceeds to all, as any had need. 46 Day by day, as they spent much time together in the temple, they broke bread at home and ate their food with glad and generous hearts, 47 praising God and having the goodwill of all the people. And day by day the Lord added to their number those who were being saved.

Acts 3:11–26

11 While he clung to Peter and John, all the people ran together to them in the portico called Solomon's Portico, utterly astonished. 12 When Peter saw it, he addressed the people, "You Israelites, why do you wonder at this, or why do you stare at us, as though by our own power or piety we had made him walk? 13 The God of Abraham, the God of Isaac, and the God of Jacob, the God of our ancestors has glorified his servant Jesus, whom you handed over and rejected in the presence of Pilate, though he had decided to release him. 14 But you rejected the Holy and Righteous One and asked to have a murderer given to you, 15 and you killed the Author of life, whom God raised from the dead. To this we are witnesses. 16 And by faith in his name, his name itself has made this man strong, whom you see and know; and the faith that is through Jesus has given

him this perfect health in the presence of all of you.

17 "And now, friends, I know that you acted in ignorance, as did also your rulers. 18 In this way God fulfilled what he had foretold through all the prophets, that his Messiah would suffer. 19 Repent therefore, and turn to God so that your sins may be wiped out, 20 so that times of refreshing may come from the presence of the Lord, and that he may send the Messiah appointed for you, that is, Jesus, 21 who must remain in heaven until the time of universal restoration that God announced long ago through his holy prophets. 22 Moses said, 'The Lord your God will raise up for you from your own people a prophet like me. You must listen to whatever he tells you. 23 And it will be that everyone who does not listen to that prophet will be utterly rooted out of the people.' 24 And all the prophets, as many as have spoken, from Samuel and those after him, also predicted these days. 25 You are the descendants of the prophets and of the covenant that God gave to your ancestors, saying to Abraham, 'And in your descendants all the families of the earth shall be blessed.' 26 When God raised up his servant, he sent him first to you, to bless you by turning each of you from your wicked ways."

Acts 7:1–53
7 Then the high priest asked him, "Are these things so?"

2 And Stephen replied: "Brothers and fathers, listen to me. The God of glory appeared to our ancestor Abraham when he was in Mesopotamia, before he lived in Haran, 3 and said to him, 'Leave your country and your relatives and go to the land that I will show you.' 4 Then he left the country of the Chaldeans and settled in Haran. After his father died, God had him move from there to this country in which you are now living. 5 He did not give him any of it as a heritage, not even a foot's length, but promised to give it to him as his possession and to his descendants after him, even though he had no child. 6 And God spoke in these terms, that his descendants would be resident aliens in a country belonging to others, who would enslave them and mistreat them during four hundred years. 7 'But I will judge the nation that they serve,' said God, 'and after that they shall come out and worship me in this place.' 8 Then he gave him the covenant of circumcision. And so Abraham became the father of Isaac and circumcised him on the eighth day; and Isaac became the father of Jacob, and Jacob of the twelve patriarchs. 9 "The patriarchs, jealous of Joseph, sold him into Egypt; but God was with him, 10 and rescued him from all his afflictions, and enabled him to win favor and to show wisdom when he stood before Pharaoh, king of Egypt, who appointed him ruler over Egypt and over all his household. 11 Now there came a famine throughout Egypt and Canaan, and great suffering, and our ancestors could find no food. 12 But when Jacob heard that there was grain in Egypt, he sent our ancestors there on their first visit. 13 On the second visit Joseph made himself known to his brothers, and Joseph's family became known to Pharaoh. 14 Then Joseph sent and invited his father Jacob and all his relatives to come to him, seventy-five in all; 15 so Jacob went down to Egypt. He himself died there as well as our ancestors, 16 and their bodies were brought back to Shechem and laid in the tomb that Abraham had bought for a sum of silver from the sons of Hamor in

Shechem.

17 "But as the time drew near for the fulfillment of the promise that God had made to Abraham, our people in Egypt increased and multiplied 18 until another king who had not known Joseph ruled over Egypt. 19 He dealt craftily with our race and forced our ancestors to abandon their infants so that they would die. 20 At this time Moses was born, and he was beautiful before God. For three months he was brought up in his father's house; 21 and when he was abandoned, Pharaoh's daughter adopted him and brought him up as her own son. 22 So Moses was instructed in all the wisdom of the Egyptians and was powerful in his words and deeds.

23 "When he was forty years old, it came into his heart to visit his relatives, the Israelites. 24 When he saw one of them being wronged, he defended the oppressed man and avenged him by striking down the Egyptian. 25 He supposed that his kinsfolk would understand that God through him was rescuing them, but they did not understand. 26 The next day he came to some of them as they were quarreling and tried to reconcile them, saying, 'Men, you are brothers; why do you wrong each other?' 27 But the man who was wronging his neighbor pushed Moses aside, saying, 'Who made you a ruler and a judge over us? 28 Do you want to kill me as you killed the Egyptian yesterday?' 29 When he heard this, Moses fled and became a resident alien in the land of Midian. There he became the father of two sons.

30 "Now when forty years had passed, an angel appeared to him in the wilderness of Mount Sinai, in the flame of a burning bush. 31 When Moses saw it, he was amazed at the sight; and as he approached to look, there came the voice of the Lord: 32 'I am the God of your ancestors, the God of Abraham, Isaac, and Jacob.' Moses began to tremble and did not dare to look. 33 Then the Lord said to him, 'Take off the sandals from your feet, for the place where you are standing is holy ground. 34 I have surely seen the mistreatment of my people who are in Egypt and have heard their groaning, and I have come down to rescue them. Come now, I will send you to Egypt.'

35 "It was this Moses whom they rejected when they said, 'Who made you a ruler and a judge?' and whom God now sent as both ruler and liberator through the angel who appeared to him in the bush. 36 He led them out; having performed wonders and signs in Egypt, at the Red Sea, and in the wilderness for forty years. 37 This is the Moses who said to the Israelites, 'God will raise up a prophet for you from your own people as he raised me up.' 38 He is the one who was in the congregation in the wilderness with the angel who spoke to him at Mount Sinai, and with our ancestors; and he received living oracles to give to us. 39 Our ancestors were unwilling to obey him; instead, they pushed him aside, and in their hearts they turned back to Egypt, 40 saying to Aaron, 'Make gods for us who will lead the way for us; as for this Moses who led us out from the land of Egypt, we do not know what has happened to him.' 41 At that time they made a calf, offered a sacrifice to the idol, and reveled in the works of their hands. 42 But God turned away from them and handed them over to worship the host of heaven, as it is written in the book of the prophets:

'Did you offer to me slain victims and sacrifices
    forty years in the wilderness, O house of Israel?

43 No; you took along the tent of Moloch,
   and the star of your god Rephan,
      the images that you made to worship;
so I will remove you beyond Babylon.'
44 "Our ancestors had the tent of testimony in the wilderness, as God directed when he spoke to Moses, ordering him to make it according to the pattern he had seen. 45 Our ancestors in turn brought it in with Joshua when they dispossessed the nations that God drove out before our ancestors. And it was there until the time of David, 46 who found favor with God and asked that he might find a dwelling place for the house of Jacob. 47 But it was Solomon who built a house for him. 48 Yet the Most High does not dwell in houses made with human hands; as the prophet says,
49 'Heaven is my throne,
   and the earth is my footstool.
What kind of house will you build for me, says the Lord,
   or what is the place of my rest?
50 Did not my hand make all these things?'

51 "You stiff-necked people, uncircumcised in heart and ears, you are forever opposing the Holy Spirit, just as your ancestors used to do. 52 Which of the prophets did your ancestors not persecute? They killed those who foretold the coming of the Righteous One, and now you have become his betrayers and murderers. 53 You are the ones that received the law as ordained by angels, and yet you have not kept it."

Acts 10:34–43

34 Then Peter began to speak to them: "I truly understand that God shows no partiality, 35 but in every nation anyone who fears him and does what is right is acceptable to him. 36 You know the message he sent to the people of Israel, preaching peace by Jesus Christ—he is Lord of all. 37 That message spread throughout Judea, beginning in Galilee after the baptism that John announced: 38 how God anointed Jesus of Nazareth with the Holy Spirit and with power; how he went about doing good and healing all who were oppressed by the devil, for God was with him. 39 We are witnesses to all that he did both in Judea and in Jerusalem. They put him to death by hanging him on a tree; 40 but God raised him on the third day and allowed him to appear, 41 not to all the people but to us who were chosen by God as witnesses, and who ate and drank with him after he rose from the dead. 42 He commanded us to preach to the people and to testify that he is the one ordained by God as judge of the living and the dead. 43 All the prophets testify about him that everyone who believes in him receives forgiveness of sins through his name."

Acts 13:13–41

13 Then Paul and his companions set sail from Paphos and came to Perga in Pamphylia. John, however, left them and returned to Jerusalem; 14 but they went on from Perga and came to Antioch in Pisidia. And on the Sabbath day they went into the synagogue and

sat down. 15 After the reading of the law and the prophets, the officials of the synagogue sent them a message, saying, "Brothers, if you have any word of exhortation for the people, give it." 16 So Paul stood up and with a gesture began to speak:

"You Israelites, and others who fear God, listen. 17 The God of this people Israel chose our ancestors and made the people great during their stay in the land of Egypt, and with uplifted arm he led them out of it. 18 For about forty years he put up with them in the wilderness. 19 After he had destroyed seven nations in the land of Canaan, he gave them their land as an inheritance 20 for about four hundred fifty years. After that he gave them judges until the time of the prophet Samuel. 21 Then they asked for a king; and God gave them Saul son of Kish, a man of the tribe of Benjamin, who reigned for forty years. 22 When he had removed him, he made David their king. In his testimony about him he said, 'I have found David, son of Jesse, to be a man after my heart, who will carry out all my wishes.' 23 Of this man's posterity God has brought to Israel a Savior, Jesus, as he promised; 24 before his coming John had already proclaimed a baptism of repentance to all the people of Israel. 25 And as John was finishing his work, he said, 'What do you suppose that I am? I am not he. No, but one is coming after me; I am not worthy to untie the thong of the sandals on his feet.'

26 "My brothers, you descendants of Abraham's family, and others who fear God, to us the message of this salvation has been sent. 27 Because the residents of Jerusalem and their leaders did not recognize him or understand the words of the prophets that are read every Sabbath, they fulfilled those words by condemning him. 28 Even though they found no cause for a sentence of death, they asked Pilate to have him killed. 29 When they had carried out everything that was written about him, they took him down from the tree and laid him in a tomb. 30 But God raised him from the dead; 31 and for many days he appeared to those who came up with him from Galilee to Jerusalem, and they are now his witnesses to the people. 32 And we bring you the good news that what God promised to our ancestors 33 he has fulfilled for us, their children, by raising Jesus; as also it is written in the second psalm,

'You are my Son;
   today I have begotten you.'

34 As to his raising him from the dead, no more to return to corruption, he has spoken in this way,

'I will give you the holy promises made to David.'

35 Therefore he has also said in another psalm,

'You will not let your Holy One experience corruption.'

36 For David, after he had served the purpose of God in his own generation, died, waslaid beside his ancestors, and experienced corruption; 37 but he whom God raised up experienced no corruption. 38 Let it be known to you therefore, my brothers, that through this man forgiveness of sins is proclaimed to you; 39 by this Jesus everyone who believes is set free from all those sins from which you could not be freed by the law of Moses. 40 Beware, therefore, that what the prophets said does not happen to you:
41 'Look, you scoffers!

> Be amazed and perish,
> for in your days I am doing a work,
> > a work that you will never believe, even if someone tells you.'"

Romans 9:1–8

9 I am speaking the truth in Christ—I am not lying; my conscience confirms it by the Holy Spirit— 2 I have great sorrow and unceasing anguish in my heart. 3 For I could wish that I myself were accursed and cut off from Christ for the sake of my own people, my kindred according to the flesh. 4 They are Israelites, and to them belong the adoption, the glory, the covenants, the giving of the law, the worship, and the promises; 5 to them belong the patriarchs, and from them, according to the flesh, comes the Messiah, who is over all, God blessed forever. Amen.

6 It is not as though the word of God had failed. For not all Israelites truly belong to Israel, 7 and not all of Abraham's children are his true descendants; but "It is through Isaac that descendants shall be named for you." 8 This means that it is not the children of the flesh who are the children of God, but the children of the promise are counted as descendants.

Romans 9:30–33

30 What then are we to say? Gentiles, who did not strive for righteousness, have attained it, that is, righteousness through faith; 31 but Israel, who did strive for the righteousness that is based on the law, did not succeed in fulfilling that law. 32 Why not? Because they did not strive for it on the basis of faith, but as if it were based on works. They have stumbled over the stumbling stone, 33 as it is written,

> "See, I am laying in Zion a stone that will make people stumble, a rock that will make them fall,
> > and whoever believes in him will not be put to shame."

Romans 10:1–4

10 Brothers and sisters, my heart's desire and prayer to God for them is that they may be saved. 2 I can testify that they have a zeal for God, but it is not enlightened. 3 For, being ignorant of the righteousness that comes from God, and seeking to establish their own, they have not submitted to God's righteousness. 4 For Christ is the end of the law so that there may be righteousness for everyone who believes.

Romans 11:25–27

25 So that you may not claim to be wiser than you are, brothers and sisters,[a] I want you to understand this mystery: a hardening has come upon part of Israel, until the full number of the Gentiles has come in. 26 And so all Israel will be saved; as it is written,

> "Out of Zion will come the Deliverer;
> > he will banish ungodliness from Jacob."

27 "And this is my covenant with them,
   when I take away their sins."

1 Corinthians 15:1–6
15 Now I would remind you, brothers and sisters, of the good news that I proclaimed to you, which you in turn received, in which also you stand, 2 through which also you are being saved, if you hold firmly to the message that I proclaimed to you—unless you have come to believe in vain.

3 For I handed on to you as of first importance what I in turn had received: that Christ died for our sins in accordance with the scriptures, 4 and that he was buried, and that he was raised on the third day in accordance with the scriptures, 5 and that he appeared to Cephas, then to the twelve. 6 Then he appeared to more than five hundred brothers and sisters at one time, most of whom are still alive, though some have died.

Ephesians 2:11–3:13
11 So then, remember that at one time you Gentiles by birth, called "the uncircumcision" by those who are called "the circumcision"—a physical circumcision made in the flesh by human hands— 12 remember that you were at that time without Christ, being aliens from the commonwealth of Israel, and strangers to the covenants of promise, having no hope and without God in the world. 13 But now in Christ Jesus you who once were far off have been brought near by the blood of Christ. 14 For he is our peace; in his flesh he has made both groups into one and has broken down the dividing wall, that is, the hostility between us. 15 He has abolished the law with its commandments and ordinances, that he might create in himself one new humanity in place of the two, thus making peace, 16 and might reconcile both groups to God in one body through the cross, thus putting to death that hostility through it. 17 So he came and proclaimed peace to you who were far off and peace to those who were near; 18 for through him both of us have access in one Spirit to the Father. 19 So then you are no longer strangers and aliens, but you are citizens with the saints and also members of the household of God, 20 built upon the foundation of the apostles and prophets, with Christ Jesus himself as the cornerstone. 21 In him the whole structure is joined together and grows into a holy temple in the Lord; 22 in whom you also are built together spiritually into a dwelling place for God.

3 This is the reason that I Paul am a prisoner for Christ Jesus for the sake of you Gentiles— 2 for surely you have already heard of the commission of God's grace that was given me for you, 3 and how the mystery was made known to me by revelation, as I wrote above in a few words, 4 a reading of which will enable you to perceive my understanding of the mystery of Christ. 5 In former generations this mystery was not made known to humankind, as it has now been revealed to his holy apostles and prophets by the Spirit: 6 that is, the Gentiles have become fellow heirs, members of the same body, and sharers in the promise in Christ Jesus through the gospel.

7 Of this gospel I have become a servant according to the gift of God's grace that was given me by the working of his power. 8 Although I am the very least of all the saints, this grace was given to me to bring to the Gentiles the news of the boundless riches of Christ, 9 and to make everyone see what is the plan of the mystery hidden for ages in God who created all things; 10 so that through the church the wisdom of God in its rich variety might now be made known to the rulers and authorities in the heavenly places. 11 This was in accordance with the eternal purpose that he has carried out in Christ Jesus our Lord, 12 in whom we have access to God in boldness and confidence through faith in him. 13 I pray therefore that you may not lose heart over my sufferings for you; they are your glory.

Ephesians 4:1–16

4 I therefore, the prisoner in the Lord, beg you to lead a life worthy of the calling to which you have been called, 2 with all humility and gentleness, with patience, bearing with one another in love, 3 making every effort to maintain the unity of the Spirit in the bond of peace. 4 There is one body and one Spirit, just as you were called to the one hope of your calling, 5 one Lord, one faith, one baptism, 6 one God and Father of all, who is above all and through all and in all.

7 But each of us was given grace according to the measure of Christ's gift. 8 Therefore it is said,
"When he ascended on high he made captivity itself a captive;
    he gave gifts to his people."
9 (When it says, "He ascended," what does it mean but that he had also descended into the lower parts of the earth? 10 He who descended is the same one who ascended far above all the heavens, so that he might fill all things.) 11 The gifts he gave were that some would be apostles, some prophets, some evangelists, some pastors and teachers, 12 to equip the saints for the work of ministry, for building up the body of Christ, 13 until all of us come to the unity of the faith and of the knowledge of the Son of God, to maturity, to the measure of the full stature of Christ. 14 We must no longer be children, tossed to and fro and blown about by every wind of doctrine, by people's trickery, by their craftiness in deceitful scheming. 15 But speaking the truth in love, we must grow up in every way into him who is the head, into Christ, 16 from whom the whole body joined and knit together by every ligament with which it is equipped, as each part is working properly, promotes the body's growth in building itself up in love.

1 Peter 2:1–10

Rid yourselves, therefore, of all malice, and all guile, insincerity, envy, and all slander. 2 Like newborn infants, long for the pure, spiritual milk, so that by it you may grow into salvation— 3 if indeed you have tasted that the Lord is good.

4 Come to him, a living stone, though rejected by mortals yet chosen and precious in God's sight and 5 like living stones, let yourselves be built into a spiritual house, to be a holy priesthood, to offer spiritual sacrifices acceptable to God through Jesus Christ. 6

For it stands in scripture:
"See, I am laying in Zion a stone,
   a cornerstone chosen and precious;
and whoever believes in him will not be put to shame."
7 To you then who believe, he is precious; but for those who do not believe,
"The stone that the builders rejected
   has become the very head of the corner,"
8 and "A stone that makes them stumble,
   and a rock that makes them fall."
They stumble because they disobey the word, as they were destined to do.
9 But you are a chosen race, a royal priesthood, a holy nation, God's own people, in order that you may proclaim the mighty acts of him who called you out of darkness into his marvelous light.
10 Once you were not a people,
   but now you are God's people;
once you had not received mercy,
   but now you have received mercy.

APPENDIX C: MAP OF ABRAHAM'S JOURNEY

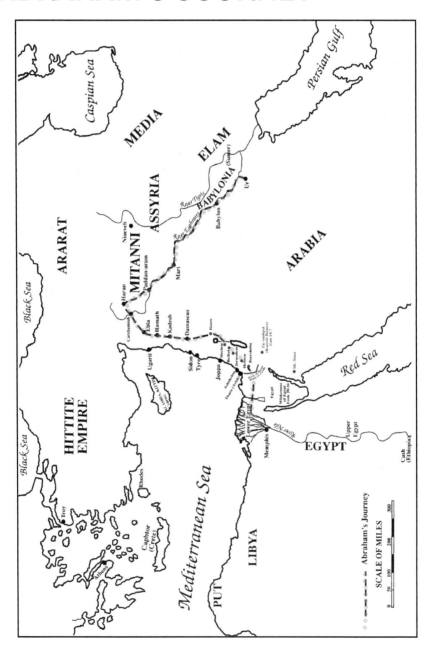